"Judy's excellent book, *When You Love* [...] practical help to those who have prodigals, it is a preparation for the ministry God will give you in helping others who are parents of prodigals. This book, because it is biblically based, will help you comfort others with the comfort, wisdom, and understanding you will receive from Judy and Steve's experience. O Beloved, don't waste your sorrows—share how God has sustained you. Share what you've learned from loving a prodigal."

—Kay Arthur, author, Bible teacher

"So many times those who pray for and love the wayward feel utterly alone, but in *When You Love a Prodigal*, you will find needed solace and companionship. Backed by Scripture, real-life experience, and hard-won wisdom, author Judy Douglass has the expertise and heart to guide you through a devotional prayer journey toward hope. In its pages you will begin to understand what a gift it is to your walk with God to labor in prayer for another."

—Mary DeMuth, author of *Healing Every Day: A 90-Day Devotional Journey*

"As a friend of mine used to say, 'Motherhood is hard,' and every mother I know agrees. Somehow, women survive, but it is not easy. Some parents who have children of their own reach out to children who have no home. Such has been the case with Steve and Judy Douglass. I have known them for years, long before they were married. I would trust them with my life. God trusted them with an abandoned child, and they took him in and loved him as their own. There is no doubt they saved his life. It was not easy. Her story is amazing. Judy shares biblical truths she learned on her agonizing journey that will be helpful to anyone who loves a prodigal."

—Mary Graham, former president, Women of Faith

"Thank you, Judy, for the gift of *When You Love a Prodigal*. This ninety-day devotional invites us to enter a journey of hope and in so doing experience the very character of a loving heavenly Father who welcomes and restores prodigals. This compelling book is written from the heart and full of encouragement!"

—Dr. Crawford W. Loritts Jr., author, speaker, radio host;
senior pastor, Fellowship Bible Church, Roswell, GA

"*When You Love a Prodigal* is a gold mine of honesty, compassion, hope, and encouragement. If you love a prodigal, this is *the* book to read!"

—Josh and Dottie McDowell, author/speaker, Cru

"Every parent of a prodigal benefits from the presence of a friend who has stood in the road searching in the distance for a glimpse of their loved one's return. Judy Douglass is just such a friend. With mounds of wisdom and with worn knees, Judy offers the comfort of companionship. God has placed Judy on a platform of worldwide leadership, and yet she bends close to every single parent who suffers."

—Elisa Morgan, speaker; author, *The Beauty of Broken*
and *Hello, Beauty Full*; cohost, *Discover the Word*;
president emerita, MOPS International

"This book is a book of *hope*. Each day brings a huge dose of powerful, faith-building encouragement through God's Word. The stories, uplifting insights, and Judy's personal journey will give you courage to face another day, changing your fear to faith. Each devotional points you to your heavenly Father, who hears your cries and answers your prayers. He loves you and He loves your prodigal. Don't give up, no matter what!"

—Fern Nichols, founder, Moms in Prayer International

"Judy Douglass has written a beautiful, profound, and personal exploration of the power of truly accepting love. It will move every reader, because each of us must be loved as a prodigal if we are to be loved at all."

—Nancy and John Ortberg, senior pastor, Menlo Church

"My wife and I had the privilege and joy of working closely with Judy and her husband as they were walking through the challenges of loving a prodigal. I am so pleased that the powerful lessons Judy learned on her journey of obedience and service will bless so many who are also seeking to love their prodigals well."

—Roy Peterson, president, American Bible Society; former president, Seed Company and Wycliffe Bible Translators

"Loving a prodigal, without enabling a child, is one of *the* most challenging assignments a parent ever faces. If there is ever a time parents need a mentor, it's when one of their children goes rogue. Judy Douglass is the compassionate mentor and friend you need to guide you as parents in loving your child."

—Dennis and Barbara Rainey, cofounders of FamilyLife

"As parents of a prodigal child, the journey to unconditional love and forgiveness for Judy and Steve Douglass came in understanding God's unfailing grace for their child . . . and themselves. Let this book of devotionals so honestly and beautifully written by Judy encourage and sustain you as you walk your path to bring your prodigal home. You don't have to walk it alone."

—Les Steckel, former CEO and president, Fellowship of Christian Athletes

WHEN YOU
LOVE
A PRODIGAL

WHEN YOU
LOVE
A PRODIGAL

90 Days of Grace for the Wilderness

Judy Douglass

BETHANYHOUSE
a division of Baker Publishing Group
Minneapolis, Minnesota

Published by Bethany House Publishers
11400 Hampshire Avenue South
Bloomington, Minnesota 55438
www.bethanyhouse.com

Bethany House Publishers is a division of
Baker Publishing Group, Grand Rapids, Michigan

Printed in the United States of America

Library of Congress Cataloging-in-Publication Data
Names: Douglass, Judy Downs, author.
Title: When you love a prodigal : 90 days of grace for the wilderness / Judy Douglass.
Description: Bloomington : Bethany House Publishers, [2019] | Includes bibliographical references.
Identifiers: LCCN 2019018621| ISBN 9780764233944 (trade paper) | ISBN 9781493420087 (ebk.)
Subjects: LCSH: Parenting—Religious aspects—Christianity. | Parent and teenager—Religious aspects—Christianity. | Parent and child—Religious aspects—Christianity. | Parents of problem children—Religious life. | Families—Religious aspects—Christianity.
Classification: LCC BV4529 .D685 2019 | DDC 248.8/45—dc23
LC record available at https://lccn.loc.gov/2019018621

19 20 21 22 23 24 25   7 6 5 4 3 2 1

To Josh

Who God
Rescued from abandonment and loss
Relentlessly pursued as His child
Gave to us as a treasured gift
Made a teacher for us to learn the reality of grace

To the Prayer for Prodigals Community

Who walked and wept and prayed with us
on a long wilderness journey

Prodigal
Original meaning (adj.): Extravagant, lavish, abundant, and bountiful.

Recent additional meaning (n.): A person who is extravagantly wasteful, lavishly reckless, abundantly profligate.

Lover of Prodigals
(n.): One who extravagantly and lavishly, with perseverance, loves a prodigal.

Contents

Foreword

And he arose and came to his father. But *while he was still a long way off*, his father saw him and felt compassion, and ran and embraced him and kissed him.

Luke 15:20 ESV, emphasis added

A long way off. A chasm of shame and guilt and regret and anger and bitterness and despair . . . a chasm that only love and grace can navigate.

Jesus, the teacher of all teachers, teaches us. To love prodigals. To love in a way that crosses the chasm. While the prodigal is still a very, very long way off.

Jesus doesn't minimize the distance, He resources it. Fuel for the journey, fire for the soul.

Traversing the pain-filled, doubt-littered, fear-exploding route of redemption.

A son . . . two sons—one consumed with pleasure, the other consumed by the pursuit of power and control. Both prodigals. Both lost and demanding. Both a burden.

Enter the love of a father. The Father.

Yes, God loves first. And His love isn't restricted to saints—no, it focuses precisely on sinners. With sacrifice, humility, and passion.

God's love for sinners is why He loves me. A prodigal. Sure, more politely prodigal than some, but a prodigal nonetheless. The "prodigal journey" is all of our journeys.

The message of hope and life comes from the love of Jesus. God's messenger and message to prodigals.

Our reaction to the message: We dismissed and despised Him. We mocked and rejected Him. This is often what happens to those who love a prodigal.

Yet, our pain has a companion in Jesus. We're never alone in the journey across the chasm. Through the vast and tiring odyssey. In the middle of hopelessness and pain. Jesus is our guide and our friend. He is our breath and our advocate.

And in the journey, tears water the dust of discouragement. When our resolve is extinguished, and our courage depleted . . . God, through Jesus, shows us the way. "While he was still a long way off."

Jesus doesn't simply join us in the journey. No, this is His journey that He invites us to be a part of. This is His burden to carry, His wound to salve, His tear to wipe. Indeed, He knows the wilderness well.

And that is why Judy Douglass wrote this devotional. As a cup of cold water in the wilderness . . . from here to there, across the lonely and difficult chasm.

Her story is raw and personal. It's authentic and tender. Her wilderness journey has a name, a face, an aching heart. And as Judy penned the words that follow, she attacked the lie that those who cross the chasm go alone. No, you are never alone . . . because Jesus, our King and Redeemer, saw, felt compassion, ran, embraced, and kissed a desperately lost son. Our son. Our daughter. Us.

When You Love a Prodigal is a book that Jesus wrote long ago. And I'm so grateful that Judy Douglass has powerfully and compassionately highlighted the immensity and persistence of God's amazing love and grace.

—Dan Wolgemuth, president, Youth for Christ

Introduction

Wilderness

The LORD your God, who is going before you, will fight for you . . . in the wilderness. There you saw how the LORD your God carried you, as a father carries his son, all the way you went until you reached this place.

Deuteronomy 1:30–31

There were four of them, clad in orange jumpsuits, hands and feet manacled, shuffling into the courtroom. All in their late teens, they looked down, avoiding eyes, exuding pain and shame more than anger or defiance.

Ours was third in line. He looked for us, then turned away. My tears came—I couldn't stop them. That was my son, chained and imprisoned.

He had just spent two nights in the Juvenile Detention Center (JDC) because of a poor choice—a choice that led to a dangerous situation for him and my husband.

The police came and he ran; they caught him and took him to lockup. Hours later, in the middle of the night, he called, begging us to come rescue him. But we couldn't even if we wanted to. He had to stay until his hearing, two days later.

At the hearing a trial date was set, and Joshua was released to us.

Would You Take This Boy?

Seven years earlier, we had just moved to Florida. A new friend said one day, "Do you know someone who would take an eight-year-old boy?"

Those words changed my life.

My friend Carol was asking on behalf of her best friends, whose grandson had been taken from his mother because of neglect.

Joshua had a difficult start in life.

This boy had spent most of his eight years with his mom in their little trailer, surrounded by alcohol, drugs, neglect, abuse, danger. The only consistency in his life had been his grandparents, but they didn't see how they could keep him, as they were already raising his fourteen-year-old half sister.

So social services was looking for a foster home. Carol and the grandparents wanted it to be a safe, Christian home. Would it be our home? The word for us, from God, was yes.

It took almost a year before we were approved and nine-year-old Josh, almost ten, joined our two girls, ten and twelve, to complete our family.

I'm not sure who experienced the greatest shock.

For Josh: Regular bedtime. Restrictions on TV content. School every day. Church every week. Regular real meals at a table. Discipline.

For us: Noise and chaos. Mess. A boy who was barely able to read and write. Center-of-attention need. Hoarding. Fetal alcohol syndrome residuals: attention deficit disorder, learning disability, lack of cause-and-effect reasoning.

As his parents, we were far from perfect, but we made great efforts to love and care for Josh and integrate him into our family—sports, new friends, birthday parties, family activities, vacation with extended family, spiritual input, tutoring, appropriate limits.

But nothing would overcome his belief that we didn't really love him. He was sure we would eventually reject him, and he gave us plenty of reasons to do just that. He did not attach to us, and we developed only minimal emotional attachment to him.

After three years, when the county terminated his mother's rights and placed him for adoption, my husband, daughters, and I had a decision to make: Would we adopt Josh?

He didn't seem to care, but he didn't see a better option, so he was willing.

But were we?

Emotionally, it was difficult—did we want to sign up for a lifetime of the challenges Josh presented? Again, the clear answer for us was yes. And surely, we hoped, the certainty that we would not abandon him, that we were committed to love and care for him, would bring some peace and security to him.

So we all said "I do," and Josh became our son.

The next week he entered middle school. Almost thirteen and a big boy, he towered over most of the sixth-graders . . . and discovered there was power in size. Read: bully.

School was a challenge. Sitting still all day in a classroom was not possible. Teachers couldn't teach with him in the room, so he spent most days in an alternative classroom. His grades suffered. I became friends with his counselor, the vice principal, and even the principal. Seventh grade was worse. He was banned from the bus and he joined a gang.

My husband and I tried so many ways to help Josh: with school work, creative parenting approaches, counseling, youth group, sports, camp. Nothing seemed to work—he wouldn't let us help him. When the school threatened to expel him, we took a desperate step.

We placed Josh in a nearby residential program for troubled teens. It was a lifesaver, though very difficult for him and for us.

Josh was safe, living with strict rules and consequences. He studied at his own pace, filled his head with Scriptures, did many chores, received counseling—even had fun. And he was forced to relate to us—to the whole family.

The high point of his year and a half there—June 2, 1997—was the night he committed his life to Christ.

It was also the night Josh was truly born in my heart as my son.

I had loved Josh over the years. I had given him abundant time and attention. But that night, as I thanked God for Josh's decision, I had a dramatic experience. I sensed that God was giving to me *His* very own love for Josh.

Oh, how I would need that love in the years ahead!

Josh came home from the program and did well for six months. We continued at home the school curriculum he had been doing and caught him up to grade level. He begged to return to school. With trepidation and many requirements, we said yes. It was only a few weeks before he was back with his old friends. And now he had a driver's license and the freedom it provided.

We returned to homeschooling, which meant he eventually graduated. But the next six years were nightmarish. Summarizing: cars, girls, inappropriate Internet sites, drugs, alcohol, traffic tickets, juvenile detention, criminal mischief, job-hopping, stealing, serious accidents, gang fights.

I lived in dread of late-night phone calls: Would it be the hospital or the jail? We got calls from both.

Three times after he turned eighteen his actions at home meant he had made a choice to move out. Each time he came back repentant and reformed. For a while. God repeatedly brought special men into his life. Their influence continues today. But changes then were short-lived, and the old lifestyle beckoned.

Be assured, we were not always the best parents during this time. We made many mistakes.

The amazing thing is that he continued a relationship with us. But the question remained: Would he survive, or would death or jail be his likely future?

Desperate for Help

In the depths of our struggle, and recognizing we needed a lot of help, we called on friends around the world for a June 2 Worldwide Day of Prayer for Josh. We invited those we knew who were prayer warriors or experienced in such a wilderness journey to join us in focused prayer for our son. God gave us some specific answers in response to those prayers.

I would like to say we saw immediate true and total turnaround, but we didn't. We did see evidence of God's hand in Joshua's life, and so did he. So the Worldwide Day of Prayer became an annual event every June 2, and each year more people joined with us. And each year we saw new steps in a better direction for our son, though often they didn't last.

We began to feel pretty selfish keeping all this prayer for our son, so we began to broaden it—and now it is a Worldwide Prodigal Prayer Day, with a growing list of several thousand people (first names only) we pray for every June 2.

It has also grown into a global virtual prayer community, called Prayer for Prodigals. In addition to our focused day of prayer on June 2, throughout the year we have active, ongoing care and prayer online. Members must be invited in to ensure safety and privacy for sharing vulnerable personal requests. Many pray for the requests, and quite a few bless all the others by writing out their prayers.

Each year we have a theme for the prayer day. The Lord enabled me to write eight to ten mini-devotionals for each theme to prepare our hearts to pray effectively. Those devotionals, plus the dozens of other letters I have written to the community, provide much of the content for this book. Because they were originally written as letters, you will sense the personal touch, the vulnerability of chatting with friends, a mixture of stories and Scripture.

This is not a how-to book. It is a journey-together book.

There are ninety essays—ninety days of perspective on what God offers to us as we love our prodigals. At the end of each brief essay, response questions will help you process what God is saying to you. You can work through it day by day or you can read it straight through.

Loving a prodigal isn't easy, whether it's your own child, a sibling, a grandchild, a niece or nephew, a friend, a spouse, or even a parent. When someone you love veers off a safe path and makes destructive life decisions, you grow concerned. You seek to encourage better choices, point out the risks and dangers, and coax them back from harm's way.

And when those prodigal choices continue over years, you—the one who loves this prodigal—can grow desperate, thinking that nothing makes a difference. Fear escalates. Faith dwindles. Hope wanes. What can you do?

Many do what I did—pray! And ask others to pray. For we believe that God can change things, bring that prodigal home, restore sanity. And He can. But He is committed to honoring free will and wooing the prodigal back with love and grace, not force. He is patient—and He knows what it will take to win the heart and mind of your loved one.

You will ask for help, for wisdom, for advice. You will be told to set boundaries, to practice tough love, and to make sure you don't enable that prodigal.

These are good things, but I think God has given us a higher priority in His model. He has focused most often on love, mercy, and grace—in His dealings with Israel, His restoration of individuals, in the life and death of His Son, and in the story of the prodigal son.

In my own life I have not experienced judgment and punishment from God, but rather love, mercy, and grace—over and over. In these pages you will see that boundaries and consequences are helpful and needed. But we will focus more on living out this verse from Romans: "Do you show contempt for the riches of his kindness, forbearance and patience, not realizing that God's kindness is intended to lead you to repentance?" (Romans 2:4).

So come, walk with me through this difficult but rewarding wilderness journey of loving a prodigal.

1

LOVE

We love because he first loved us.
1 John 4:19

I love my prodigal. You love your prodigal.

But often it's not easy to love a prodigal. Our love is tested and stretched. Unappreciated and questioned. Not returned—even thrown back in our face. We grow weary and discouraged.

How do we keep loving as the years unfold? What does love look like when our prodigals keep making bad choices?

We know that God's love is unconditional, unfailing, radical, sacrificial. That is the love God has always had for Josh. I knew this love was mine to love Josh with, but I couldn't consistently access it.

This I know: I am not capable of that kind of love in my own strength. Jesus set an impossibly high standard. So how do we love and keep on loving our often hard-to-love prodigals?

DAY 1: He Loved Us First

We must learn to love our prodigals as Jesus loves. The key to comprehending this concept is this:

"We, though, are going to love—love and be loved. First we were loved, now we love. *He loved us first*" (1 John 4:19 THE MESSAGE, emphasis added).

If we are going to consider how we can radically love our prodigals, we ourselves must be certain of, confident in, and comfortable with God's love for *us*.

All of Scripture is a love letter to us. Many verses and passages declare and affirm His unfailing, everlasting love for us. Below are just a few of those scriptural affirmations, and they are for us.

"The LORD your God in your midst . . . He will rejoice over you with gladness, He will quiet you with His love, He will rejoice over you with singing" (Zephaniah 3:17 NKJV).

This verse paints a rich picture for me of God singing a love song to me, calming me, encouraging me with words of love. And oh, how often I need to hear that love song!

"The LORD appeared to us in the past, saying: 'I have loved you with an everlasting love; I have drawn you with unfailing kindness'" (Jeremiah 31:3).

I love this promise. He speaks tenderly to His people—to us. His love is everlasting—never ending, always there, forever. His love is unfailing—it will never let us down or abandon us or make a mistake. And with this everlasting, unfailing love, He draws us, calls us, woos us to himself.

"For I am convinced that neither death nor life, neither angels nor demons, neither the present nor the future, nor any powers, neither height nor depth, nor anything else in all creation, will be able to separate us from the love of God that is in Christ Jesus our Lord" (Romans 8:38–39).

Sometimes I am sure I have sinned or failed so badly that I have lost, destroyed, or canceled out God's love. How can He still love me? Yet these verses drill into our hearts and remind us of this truth: *We can't make God quit loving us.* No one else, nothing else, can separate us from that everlasting, unfailing love. Such comfort, such hope!

"For God did not give us a spirit of timidity, but one of power, love, and self-discipline" (2 Timothy 1:7 isv). There is a lot in this verse, but let's just camp on this truth: God gives us a spirit of love. Specifically, His Spirit living in us will love through us. All that amazing love we just considered is not only given *to* us, but also given *through* us.

Remember that core verse, 1 John 4:19, at the beginning of this chapter: He loved us first. Because God first lavished His love on us and sent His Spirit to live in us, He makes it possible for us to love with His love, which we surely need for our prodigals.

RESPONSE:

1. When have you been uncertain of God's love for you?
2. How do the biblical promises in this chapter build your confidence in God's love?

DAY 2: As High as the Heavens

> For as high as the heavens are above the earth,
> so great is his love for those who fear him.
> Psalm 103:11

I often read and pray Psalm 103. One morning as I read the verse above, I heard the Lord say, "This is what my love for you and for your prodigal looks like."

This psalm is too rich for a one-time visit, so I'm just going to get you started with some portions of it. I encourage you to go further into it with the Lord, asking what more He wants to say to you personally through it.

As you read this passage, be reminded of what God's love has done for you. Pause to remember that He says the same thing to your prodigal. When God told me this passage shows what His love for my prodigal and me looks like, I prayed that morning out of those verses that my loved one would grasp the reality and depth of God's love expressed in this psalm. I urge you to do the same.

But don't stop there. Ask God how you might demonstrate this kind of love to your very loved wanderer.

So here are portions of Psalm 103 (with verse numbers noted), followed by a few comments from what God said to me that morning:

> Praise the LORD, my soul;
> all my inmost being, praise his holy name.
> Praise the LORD, my soul,
> and forget not all his benefits—
>
> vv. 1–2

He has done so much for us, given so much to us to praise Him for, yet we so easily forget. But I don't want to forget, especially in the hard times.

> who forgives all your sins
> and heals all your diseases,
>
> v. 3

That morning, I went through this for myself, thanking Him for forgiving my many, many sins. And then, as I had no trouble recounting my prodigal's many sins, I was grateful for God's mercy toward him, as well as for the healing; I have plenty of areas of my life that need healing, but my prodigal has more parts of him that need healing than I can name. God is working on his healing too.

> who redeems your life from the pit
>> and crowns you with love and compassion,
>>> v. 4

Most of us have some acquaintance with the pit, but our prodigals seem to live there. God redeems our lives and theirs!

> who satisfies your desires with good things
>> so that your youth is renewed like the eagle's.
>>> v. 5

Too often it is our prodigals' desires for unhealthy things that send them spiraling down. May they grow to desire the good things God freely gives.

> The LORD works righteousness
>> and justice for all the oppressed.
> He made known his ways to Moses,
>> his deeds to the people of Israel:
> The LORD is compassionate and gracious,
>> slow to anger, abounding in love.
>>> vv. 6–8

Every day I am grateful that God is compassionate, gracious, slow to anger, abounding in love toward me. I pray that I can act as God does toward my loved one.

> He does not treat us as our sins deserve
>> or repay us according to our iniquities.
>>> v. 10

By this time that morning, I was on my face with gratitude that this is true. May I pay it forward with grace and mercy.

> For as high as the heavens are above the earth,
>> so great is his love for those who fear him;
>>> v. 11

There's that amazing love of God again!

> as far as the east is from the west,
>   so far has he removed our transgressions from us.
> As a father has compassion on his children,
>   so the LORD has compassion on those who fear him;
>
> vv. 12–13

Sometimes I think we need a greater measure of the Father's compassion for our prodigals.

> for he knows how we are formed,
>   he remembers that we are dust.
>
> v. 14

This is a verse I claim for myself over and over—He knows I am dust. May I remember the same is true for my prodigal. God knows we are dust, yet His love for us is higher than the heavens.

> But from everlasting to everlasting
>   the LORD's love is with those who fear him,
>   and his righteousness with their children's children—
>
> v. 17

Can you claim this? The Lord's love is with us as we fear Him, and His righteousness is with our children's children!

> with those who keep his covenant
>   and remember to obey his precepts.
> The LORD has established his throne in heaven,
>   and his kingdom rules over all.
>
> vv. 18–19

I find I must recall every day that God is on His throne in heaven—and that He rules. He will do what He says and what He wants. And what He wants is to bless us and lead us into the good He desires for us.

May God speak love and truth into your heart and mind from this psalm. May you rest in His love and live it out with your prodigal.

RESPONSE:

1. Which of the benefits of God's love for you encourages you most?
2. Which is the most difficult for you to extend to your loved one?

DAY 3: Banishing Fear

There is no fear in love. But perfect love drives out fear.
1 John 4:18

The fear can be overwhelming, can't it?

Pregnancy. Addiction. Overdose.

Wrong friends. Cutting. Suicide.

Her wasting away because she won't eat.

The call from the jail or the hospital. An accident—injuring self or others.

His doing something crazy while high. A visit from the police.

Harm to your other children. Living without God.

Your not knowing where they are or what they are doing.

Failing school. Having no future. Fear for your own life.

That's quite a list. All are quite possible, whether your prodigal is your teen or adult child, a spouse, a sibling, a parent, or a friend.

Fear can be pervasive when you love a prodigal.

I know it has been for me. Friday nights were always the worst in the darkest days of his prodigalness, because he and his friends felt it was their right to have a wild Friday night.

And even today, when he is seeking to make good choices, to choose a better life, the fear lingers and lurks: Will the past return to haunt him? Will one more hard life event trip him up again?

So how do we not live in fear? We live in love—God's love for us and for our prodigals.

Perfect love casts out fear. And only our Lord has perfect love. He *is* perfect love.

There are other things we know are true: He is God—sovereign, almighty, omnipotent, the Most High God. He is good—He does all things well, and He is always looking for ways to do good to us.

He invites us to "taste and see that the LORD is good" (Psalm 34:8).

Yes, He is love. He doesn't just love. He *is* love. And all the realities of His love—for you and me, and for our loved ones, that we have explored so far—apply here.

But bad things still happen. Wrong choices lead to painful consequences—some of which last a lifetime: People are hurt physically and emotionally, are imprisoned, have an unexpected child. Die.

So where is God's love in all those things?

We have no way of knowing all the unseen ways in which God—because of His great love—has intervened, protected, rescued. We don't know what we don't know.

But we do know that He allows us—and our prodigals—to make choices, to follow our own paths, to pursue our own desires. And sometimes those choices, paths, and desires have extreme consequences.

When I can't understand what is happening, when it seems there is no good in sight, when I feel that surely someone *did* snatch my loved one from God's hands, I can't rely on what I see or what it seems God is doing or allowing.

So I must go back to who He is: He is God. He is good. He is love. I must lean into that love, believe that His love can bring good from the worst situation and that He is able to rescue and redeem the most degenerate.

That love will cover me with grace and flood me with peace. And that love can banish my fears. And yours!

RESPONSE:

Recall a time when your prodigal's choices filled you with fear.

1. What were you afraid of? Did that fearful situation materialize?
2. Has God's love driven out fear for you? If not, how could you experience that reality?

DAY 4: Conditional or Unconditional?

But God demonstrates his own love for us in this: While we were still sinners, Christ died for us.

Romans 5:8

We humans are such a this-for-that species.

- We give a gift—with some expectation of a gift in return at the appropriate time.
- We do a favor—and even if we don't voice it, there is a hint of *you owe me* in our minds.
- We do something really sacrificially loving—and believe God will reward us.
- We give our love and our lives for those we love, especially for our children—knowing they can't even comprehend our

gift, much less repay it. And if we love a prodigal—oh, how that love is tested.

The word *unconditional* means what it says: without conditions or limitations, complete.

We all know that the love with which God loves us is called unconditional. There is no verse that I can find that uses the word *unconditional*. But we know it's true. Romans 5:8 tells us that even when we were sinful enemies of God, He loved us. And Romans 8:38–39 assures us that nothing—not even our own actions—can separate us from His love.

Thank you, Lord, for that unconditional love.

He does tell us to let His love flow through us to others, but He loves us even if we don't love others.

I have not done this easily.

Perhaps you could say the same.

For my love for my prodigal I often received attitude and back talk and experienced lack of gratitude, lies and rebellion, demands, disrespect, anger, hurtful words. Cold responses to our expressions of love. Stabs in the heart.

For me, the hard reality with my prodigal was that he felt loving me would be a betrayal of his birth mother. Over the years my love grew and gave. But could he ever say "I love you" back to me?

Please, Lord.

God's response? "Judy, unconditional love has no conditions. It does not require love in return."

It took my prodigal twelve years to say "I love you." I am grateful that now he says those words often.

Yet still I struggle with loving unconditionally. There finally came a time when there were no more abusive, hurtful words from my loved one. But then I felt unappreciated and ignored—unloved. Perhaps that's true for you too.

Again I hear, *"Unconditional love doesn't require love in return."*

Of course, without Christ, I am not capable of unconditional love—nor are you.

Which brings us back to our central verse: "We love because he first loved us" (1 John 4:19).

He gives us His unconditional love, poured out on us and in us and through us by the Holy Spirit.

Isn't that like our loving Father: He extravagantly, sacrificially, unconditionally loves us. He asks us to do the impossible—to love in the same way. Then He sends His Spirit to make the impossible possible. He enables us to love unconditionally.

What a gift for those of us who love a prodigal!

RESPONSE:

1. How has God's unconditional love become real for you?
2. When have you been challenged to keep loving in the face of your loved one's lack of love?

DAY 5: With Patience and Kindness

Love is patient, love is kind.
1 Corinthians 13:4

How could we consider what love looks like without turning to 1 Corinthians 13:4–8? Here our Lord defines love, and many of the descriptions of love apply to us and our loved ones.

First, let's examine patience and kindness.

Through my wilderness years, I developed a pretty strong commitment to loving my prodigal as Jesus loved him—and that included treating him with patience and kindness, as Paul tells us in 1 Corinthians 13. I think I became increasingly faithful to that, especially as he began making better decisions.

But there's the snag: He began making better choices, so it was *easier* for me to be patient and kind.

I think Jesus' love model calls us to be patient and kind even when our prodigals are causing us deep pain with *terrible* choices.

What Does It Look Like to Be Patient?

The word *patient* is defined as "bearing provocation, annoyance, misfortune, delay, hardship, pain, etc., with fortitude and calm and without complaint, anger, or the like."[1]

Certainly, over time, our prodigals have provided provocation, annoyance, misfortune, delay (whether waiting a few minutes or a few years), hardship, and so much pain.

Do we have fortitude? Do we stay calm and uncomplaining? Do we get angry?

Personally, I often do not respond well. I am not a patient person. I seem to have a gift to persevere, but I don't do so with patience. Even when I stay calm, even when I refrain from anger, I manage to complain—impatiently!—to my husband, or a close friend, and surely to the Lord.

What Does It Look Like to Be Kind?

I probably do better at kindness. *Kind* definitions include: "of a good or benevolent nature or disposition, as a person; having, showing, or proceeding from benevolence; considerate, or helpful; humane; gentle; loving; affectionate."[2]

I hate to see anyone hurt, so kindness is a more natural response from me, although my subtle remarks can be hurtful and unkind. Once, when my prodigal neglected to wish me a happy birthday, my response was subtly unkind.

I find it helpful, in the midst of a stressful situation, or certainly afterward, to ask myself if my behavior, words, thoughts, and attitude reflect the patience and kindness to which God has called us. Do I get annoyed or provoked? Is there anger in my voice? Are my words kind, gentle, considerate?

Unfortunately, I fail this little test too often. Fortunately, God knows I can't love with patience and kindness in my own power. I am grateful that I can ask the Holy Spirit to fill me, empower me, and even love through me. The Spirit is capable of true patience and real kindness, and He is willing and able to love through me with that supernatural power.

When I fail at loving as Christ loved—with patience and kindness—I can count on God's mercy to forgive my sin. But my loved prodigal might not be so full of grace. Rather, my lack of demonstrated love might drive him further away with genuine pain, a sense of rejection, and perhaps with him hurling an accusation of "hypocrite!" at me.

As my frustration and irritation level rises with some new offense, I remember God's patience with and kindness to me. Once again I am confounded by His love. If necessary, I ask forgiveness from God, and if I can, from my loved one.

RESPONSE:

1. What are some ways you have treated your loved one with kindness? With unkindness?
2. How has God enabled you to patiently keep loving?

DAY 6: No Record of Being Wronged

[Love] keeps no record of wrongs.
1 Corinthians 13:5

Let's continue in 1 Corinthians 13.

I did it again. Our prodigal and a friend were with us. We were telling stories—one of my favorite activities. I couldn't resist—I told not one, but two stories of bad choices he had made in the past. He did not laugh. He even looked hurt.

I asked for his forgiveness. Several times I have had to apologize for bringing up his past choices.

Clearly, I have kept some record of his wrongs. After all, I am a writer and speaker, so stories are my currency. And there is great benefit in remembering the past, learning from it, and moving into a better future.

But probably you have, as I have, let the hurt of your prodigal's choices—past or current—linger in your mind: how they have hurt, offended, and angered you. I have a mental list—sometimes even a written account—of those offenses. Some are minor irritations, others are clearly wrong, and some are deep wounds.

Perhaps you remember when

- he yelled and cursed at you.
- she lied to your face, intentionally deceitful and not at all remorseful.
- he threatened you, and how frightened you were for your other children.
- you waited up all night, not knowing where she was, what she was doing.
- you bailed him out of jail.
- the police knocked on your door to tell you about the accident she was in.

The list goes on and on.

And then there are the words you have hurled back at your loved one:

- "You always lie to me."
- "You are never responsible."
- "Will I ever be able to trust you again?"
- "You never care about anyone but yourself."

You know. You have said these words. I certainly have. These words and such thoughts reflect the reality of keeping "a record of wrongs."

Our loved prodigals wrong themselves, those who love them, and others. Sometimes those wrongs pile up and threaten to crush us. How can we trust, believe, hope? How can we forgive?

We can do so because Jesus has shown us how: He came in love and was rejected. He healed and was accused instead of thanked. He was scourged and crucified, bearing our sins, while the crowd hurled insults, soldiers beat him, and Pharisees scoffed.

And His response was, "Father, forgive them, for they do not know what they are doing" (Luke 23:34).

He could have called legions of angels. He could have destroyed them on the spot. He could have said, "I'll be back—and I'll get even."

But He didn't. He forgave them.

And that's what He asks us to do. As we let the Spirit fill us with the same love Christ has, we are freed from making our lists, from keeping a record of the way our prodigals have wronged us.

We are empowered to forgive and to truly love.

RESPONSE:

1. What is an especially painful memory for you? Do you think your prodigal intended to hurt you?
2. Does Christ's example of forgiving help you to forgive your loved one for the pain inflicted on you?

DAY 7: What Real Love Looks Like

It's amazing how many times the words *love* and *hate* are thrown around when there is a prodigal in the picture.

Most of us have heard "I hate you" more than once. And though it stings, we know it is said in the frustration of an angry moment as the most painful thing to inflict on us. But I wonder if there is another retort far more hurtful: "You don't really love me."

This can be just a barb, but it can also cause us to pause. *Why would she say that? Surely she knows I love her. Everything I do is out of my deep love.*

The Apostle Paul exhorts us to really love. Note how the New Living Translation presents these thoughts:

"Don't just pretend to love others. Really love them. Hate what is wrong. Hold tightly to what is good" (Romans 12:9).

"Dear children, let's not merely say that we love each other; let us show the truth by our actions" (1 John 3:18).

So the obvious question is, what does real love look like? How do we show this truth by our actions? Below are five thoughts on demonstrating a real love for our prodigals.

Love speaks truth. Often the first expression of love we jump to for a prodigal is "tough love." After all, we have a responsibility to provide correction and discipline to help them turn from their wicked ways. We must speak truth to them, explaining what is right and helping them understand that choices have consequences.

Scripture affirms that this is following God's example, "because the Lord disciplines the one he loves, and he chastens everyone he accepts as his son" (Hebrews 12:6).

Real love will let them experience natural consequences, or add some consequences appropriate to the choices made and the nature of our relationship with this prodigal.

But tough love is not always God's approach, nor should it always be ours.

Love gives mercy. Earlier we were reminded not to keep a record of wrongs suffered. Any list we have needs to be forgiven. But of course our prodigals keep sinning (as do we). So often, maybe even daily, there are new offenses that do not need to be put on a list but need to be forgiven.

Peter tells us this wonderful truth: "Above all, love each other deeply, because love covers over a multitude of sins" (1 Peter 4:8).

So many times I have thanked God that His love has covered my multitude of sins. Can I do no less than to forgive my loved one?

Love extends grace. Even as God has repeatedly forgiven my many sins, He has also given me grace over and over. Sometimes it is grace *instead* of the consequences I deserve, or favor with someone who could help or hurt me, or maybe it is even the strength or courage or power to do something I have not been prepared to do.

I have sought to live by words that God repeatedly affirmed as His desire for me to extend grace to my prodigal: *"When you make mistakes with this boy"*—and I made many—*"err on the side of grace."*

"And God is able to bless you abundantly, so that in all things at all times, having all that you need, you will abound in every good work" (2 Corinthians 9:8).

If God can extend that much grace to us, He can enable us to do the same toward our prodigals.

Love bestows blessing. Over the years, my loved prodigal has done many things that made me want to return in kind, to say, "See you later," to give up, to speak a curse.

Every time, God reminds me of His instruction through Peter: "Do not repay evil with evil or insult with insult. On the contrary, repay evil with blessing, because to this you were called so that you may inherit a blessing" (1 Peter 3:9).

So I have practiced speaking blessing to him, doing something kind for him, reading a blessing I have written for him. It has transformed my attitude over and over, and it has convinced him that my love for him is real.

Love confers honor. Sometimes I can start thinking I'm better than my prodigal. After all, I haven't done what he has. I walk with God fairly consistently. I keep loving him no matter what.

But God is quick to remind me of His words in Philippians: "Do nothing out of selfish ambition or vain conceit. Rather, in humility value others above yourselves, not looking to your own interests but each of you to the interests of the others" (Philippians 2:3–4).

Can we do that? Can we put aside our "better living" and not think more highly of ourselves than we do our prodigals?

Can we live out this instruction from Romans? "Be devoted to one another in love. Honor one another above yourselves" (Romans 12:10).

As always, when we understand the human impossibility of truly loving anyone—including our prodigals—the way Christ loved, we must go to our knees and say, "Yes, Lord, I need you. Please fill me with your Holy Spirit. Give me your supernatural power to love as you have loved me."

RESPONSE:

1. What did it feel like when your loved one said, "I hate you"?
2. How have you been able to show real love, as described in this devotion?

DAY 8: Love Goes to War

We have an enemy. And so do our prodigals.

- That enemy is a liar. He will say anything he needs to in order to lead our loved ones astray (John 8:44).
- That enemy is a schemer. He is tricky and sneaky—always seeking ways to divert and entrap those who so easily succumb to his ruses (Ephesians 6:11).
- That enemy has hurled curses across generations, many aimed at us and our prodigals (Revelation 12:9–12).
- That enemy is a lion. He is on the hunt, looking to devour and destroy those we love (1 Peter 5:8).

But we love, and love goes to war. Love enters the battle. Love fights.

On June 2, 1997, three significant things happened regarding our prodigal:

First, he met Jesus. He was fourteen and in a residential program. His house dad called to tell us that our son had received Christ and they had baptized him.

Second, I had the only real vision I have ever had. I could see God above me, with a vat full of something that He was pouring into me. I asked what it was. *"It's my love for Josh. You're going to need it."*

Third, that night and the two nights following I was in an intense spiritual battle. It seemed that Satan was not happy that Josh—one of his own—had been snatched from his grasp, and he was determined to keep Josh from truly following Jesus. For three nights I didn't sleep; I prayed for my son.

Then God released me from those all-night prayer vigils. But not from fighting for my son.

We began our annual June 2 Worldwide Prodigal Prayer Day because that battle grew fiercer. It has not been easily won. The evil one has not been able to snatch this boy—now a man—from God's hands. But he has wielded great influence, enticed with temptations, and sent harm and destruction his way many times.

But he will not win, not with my prodigal and not with yours. Because we love our prodigals. And love goes to war.

We are a father standing between a child and harm, the mama bear protecting her cubs, a friend indeed standing strong, a brother who has his brother's back.

We will put on our armor (Ephesians 6) and stand against the enemy. He will not defeat us or destroy our loved ones.

How do we fight?

We resist the devil (James 4:7), demolish strongholds (2 Corinthians 10:4), break the chains, and set the captives free (Isaiah 61:1–3). (We will look more thoroughly at resisting the devil in chapter 6, "Prayer.")

Of course, no matter how strong our love, we do not have the power in ourselves to win this war. But we have living in us the Power that overcame sin and raised Jesus from the dead (Romans 8:11).

As we let the Holy Spirit fill and empower us, we see—for ourselves and for our loved prodigals—the fulfillment of this promise of God's rescue through His unfailing love:

> But I trust in you, LORD;
>   I say, "You are my God."
> My times are in your hands;
>   deliver me from the hands of my enemies,
>   from those who pursue me.
> Let your face shine on your servant;
>   save me in your unfailing love.
>
> Psalm 31:14–16

RESPONSE:

1. In what ways have you seen the evil one pursue your prodigal?
2. What Scripture has been a sword for you in fighting for your prodigal?

DAY 9: Never Give Up

When our son came to our family at almost ten years old, he had experienced significant rejection and abandonment. He did not trust. He was certain that we also would reject and abandon him. And he gave us many reasons to do so.

It took more than ten years before he truly believed we were committed to him.

Why did it take so long? I'm sure there are many reasons, but two come to mind at this point: Betrayal destroys trust, and trust takes time to heal and rebuild. Our efforts to love him well seemed inadequate to overcome the past.

But we did choose to love—as God had loved us. We were guided by these challenging descriptions of real love: Love "always protects, always trusts, always hopes, always perseveres. Love never fails" (1 Corinthians 13:7–8).

These are not wishy-washy descriptions. "Always" means always. And "never" means never.

Love always protects. Surely this abandoned boy needed protection. For starters, he needed to be protected from the past, from patterns, and from himself.

- The past—things taken from him, things done to him.
- Patterns learned—how to live and love as a survivor, that no one could be trusted.
- Himself—what he believed about himself, the choices he made.

There were many other areas of concern, and we tried to provide that protection as well.

Love always trusts. We wanted to trust him, and to assure him that we trusted him. That was difficult. We sought to help him learn to live in a trustworthy way. But trust for us really meant trusting that God was always working to redeem and restore this child—that *He* was trustworthy. And over time our trust in our son would grow. (See chapter 5, "Trust.")

Love always hopes. Sometimes hope was all there was for us. Our son didn't have hope that he would make it through school, get back with his mother, know his dad, overcome his life habits, or have a future. Sometimes we despaired along with him. But God's promise of hope for a future kept us steady, hoping, and giving hope. (See chapter 8, "Hope.")

Love always perseveres. The results of his birth mother's choices while pregnant with him made school difficult for our son. We ended up homeschooling through high school, which he did not appreciate.

Each day, as I gave him school assignments, his attitude annoyed and even angered me. I would leave his room declaring to God, *"I quit. He doesn't care; why should I? I can't keep doing this."*

God always had the same response: *"So when did I give up on you, Judy?"*

And I replied, *"I know. Never. But you're God."*

"Yes, and I love this young man. I have shared that love with you, and you can do this. You can persevere in loving him."

So I did.

Love never fails. Always—and never. God's love flowing through us always protects, trusts, hopes, and perseveres. And it never fails.

I'm grateful for that, because I fail. Too often I try to love in my own power. I let the rejection of my love make me want to withdraw. I want to give up.

But God's love never fails. And He promises to love through me. Which brings us back to where we started: We love because God loved us first.

Love keeps loving. We love it when God does big miracles quickly, but we all know that He usually works over time. When you love a prodigal, you must be patient. Don't despair. Keep praying.

And keep loving your prodigal as God has loved you.

RESPONSE:

1. When have you felt like giving up on your prodigal?
2. How has God enabled you to keep on loving?

2

GRACE

Let us then approach God's throne of grace with confidence, so that
we may receive mercy and find grace to help us in our time of need.

Hebrews 4:16

Our God has much experience loving prodigals—such as you
and me and all of humanity. So He is the perfect companion
for us on this wilderness journey. He goes with us. He comforts us. He gives hope. He relieves our fears.

And He gives grace—for all our inadequacies and mistakes, and for
the pain experienced by and caused by those we love so much.

Most of us are not naturally full of grace. We don't receive it or give
it easily. It's certainly been a journey for me to understand grace.

When I met Jesus in high school, I began to get a glimpse of grace.
After all, I was saved by grace through faith.

Later, I remember looking out over the valley below Cru's California
campus one night asking, *Why me, God? Why am I so blessed, so privileged?* Another hint at grace.

Looking back over the years, I see how the grace of God protected
me from some wrong choices: He extracted me from the wrong crowd

in high school. He said that if I married the good man I was engaged to, I wouldn't be able to do what He wanted me to do. More grace.

My work, my friends, my husband, and especially my children have been effective grace instructors. Especially Josh.

So come with me and accept our Father's amazing offer to find grace in our time of need.

DAY 10: The Greatness of Grace

God has invited us into His presence. To talk with Him.

As we who love a prodigal come in prayer to God—who sits on the throne of grace!—we are so blessed. Our need is great, deep, and ongoing. But through prayer we have a means to discover the reality of God's grace in the intense crucible and classroom of life with our prodigals.

So what is grace?

In various dictionaries, it is defined with words such as *favor, goodwill, kindness, forgiveness, charity, love, mercy, clemency, pardon, leniency, reprieve.*

Sometimes seeing the antonyms also helps us understand the meaning of a word. Opposites of grace are *animosity, enmity, disfavor, harshness, disrespect, dishonor.*

But we gain even greater insight into God's definition of grace from the Greek lexicon. The Greek word for grace is *charis,* which has the same root as words for joy, thanks, and gift. Here are some definitions and descriptions:

1. grace
   a. that which affords joy, pleasure, delight, sweetness, charm, loveliness: grace of speech
2. good will, loving-kindness, favour
   a. of the merciful kindness by which God, exerting his holy influence upon souls, turns them to Christ, keeps, strengthens, increases them in Christian faith, knowledge, affection, and kindles them to the exercise of the Christian virtues

3. what is due to grace
   a. the spiritual condition of one governed by the power of divine grace
   b. the token or proof of grace, benefit
      1. a gift of grace
      2. benefit, bounty
4. thanks (for benefits, services, favours), recompense, reward[1]

Some words that have the same root, to help broaden our understanding, are *charity, charisma, charismatic.*

Grace is God's avenue for presenting gifts to us. Scripture tells us that gifts have been bestowed on us by the grace of God, delivered by the Lord Jesus, and continually poured out on us and in us by the Holy Spirit.

Some of these "grace-gifts" include:

- Sufficiency for every need (2 Corinthians 9:8)
- Redemption (Romans 3:24)
- Incomparable riches (Ephesians 2:7)
- Encouragement (2 Thessalonians 2:16)
- Strength (1 Timothy 2:2)
- Growth (2 Peter 3:18)

Taking some liberty with all that comes from the root *char,* you might say that grace is an undeserved gift from God, joyfully given and gratefully received.

My prayer is that the grace of the Lord Jesus Christ be poured out on us abundantly.

RESPONSE:

1. Which meaning of grace has been enlightening to you? In what way?
2. How have you seen the grace of God active in your life?

DAY 11: Grace Requires No Alibi

Josh Bales is a great musician. He has led worship in numerous churches in my area, as well as many concerts. I have often listened to his music in my car.

My favorite song of his is called "Only the Sinner." And my favorite line is "Only those who have no alibi . . . Jesus saves."[2]

It's a song about grace.

Those of us who love prodigals know all about alibis. Prodigals always have alibis. Or excuses. Or blame for someone else. Surely *they* didn't do it, whatever "it" is. Falsely accused. Unfairly caught. And always an alibi.

But what about us? Don't we have alibis? Excuses? What we did—or didn't do—wasn't really wrong. Little sins.

"Only those who have no alibi / Only those who cannot hide their sin . . . Jesus saves."

You see, grace is a gift. It was paid for with the incomprehensible price of the death of the Son. Then it is offered freely to you, to me, to our prodigals, to everyone.

"But the gift is not like the trespass. For if the many died by the trespass of the one man [Adam], how much more did God's grace and the gift that came by the grace of the one man, Jesus Christ, overflow to the many!" (Romans 5:15).

Grace overflows to the many. To you. To me. To our prodigals. But why do we not all *live* in that grace? Why do our loved ones not experience it?

We only access that grace as we see our *need* for it. It is a gift that must be received. If we keep offering alibis—reasons that we are worthy, proof that we are good, excuses for our little sins, with no admission of our utter neediness—then God's grace is still inaccessible, out of our reach.

It is so hard to come before our God, admitting our weakness, our impurity, our unworthiness, our vileness.

Yet it is that humbling of ourselves, confessing our sin, and turning from our own way that releases the outrageous, abundant, lavish, free grace of God to cover us, fill us, sustain us, free us, lift us, encourage us, and strengthen us.

Hard as it is, I often have to bring my alibis to the feet of Jesus. When I finally give them to Him, He pours His grace all over me.

If it is hard for *me* to give up my alibis, I'm sure it is also hard for my prodigal. And if my generous God freely gives His extravagant grace to me, how can I do less to those I love?

RESPONSE:

1. Do you have any alibis that are keeping you from living freely in God's grace?

2. Can you see ways to give grace to your prodigal to help her or him discard alibis?

DAY 12: Amazing Grace!

Perhaps you know the story. John Newton was an insubordinate sailor in the British Navy who became involved in the horrific slave trade. During a terrible storm at sea one night, he surrendered his life to Christ. He became an Anglican priest and hymn writer. His most famous hymn is "Amazing Grace."

Certainly the prodigals we love need to receive this amazing grace. But so do we. Though our rebellion may not be as visible, as destructive, or as "bad," we are *also* prodigals.

The words of this song bring tears, promote repentance, stimulate gratitude, and provide hope. With that in mind, I invite you to try the activity below with the lyrics to "Amazing Grace." It helped me see myself with God's eyes and truly appreciate again His incredible grace toward me.

First, go through the lyrics for yourself, asking God to speak to you through each phrase. Let His grace flow into your heart and mind. Ponder how this grace impacts your relationship with your gracious God. And think of how this grace can affect your relationship with your prodigal.

Amazing Grace

Amazing grace, how sweet the sound,
That saved a wretch like me.
I once was lost but now am found,
Was blind, but now I see.

'Twas grace that taught my heart to fear.
And grace, my fears relieved.
How precious did that grace appear
The hour I first believed.

Through many dangers, toils and snares
I have already come;
'Tis grace that brought me safe thus far
and grace will lead me home.

The Lord has promised good to me.
His word my hope secures.
He will my shield and portion be,
As long as life endures.

Yea, when this flesh and heart shall fail,
And mortal life shall cease,
I shall possess within the veil,
A life of joy and peace.

When we've been there ten thousand years
Bright shining as the sun,
We've no less days to sing God's praise
Than when we'd first begun.[3]

Now go through the words of the hymn again, praying through them for your loved one. Ask God to work in your prodigal as He did in John Newton. And as He has worked in you. Plead with your Father—who invites you to the throne of grace—for these truths to bring tears, promote repentance, stimulate gratitude, and provide hope for your prodigal.

RESPONSE:

1. What phrase or verse in "Amazing Grace" struck you the most?
2. What did praying this for your prodigal prompt in your heart and mind?

DAY 13: Grace Stoops

God's grace has stooped to reach us.

"We can understand someone dying for a person worth dying for, and we can understand how someone good and noble could inspire us to selfless sacrifice. But God put his love on the line for us by offering his Son in sacrificial death while we were of no use whatever to him" (Romans 5:7–8, THE MESSAGE).

Do you realize how far God had to stoop to pour out His grace on us?

. . . from heaven to earth,

. . . from God to humanity,

. . . from holiness to depravity.

Chuck Swindoll commented in an article on that same translation of Romans 5:7–8. He reminds us:

Don't miss the absence of conditions in the Romans passage above. God didn't look down and say, "When those scoundrels show the least bit of interest in cleaning up their act, then I'll meet them more than half way." No, while we were sinning and loving it, the Father stooped and extended supreme grace in the person of His Son.

He didn't ignore our sin. He didn't excuse our sin. He looked past our sin and accepted us in spite of it. And so? Let's go there on behalf of others. Embrace them in spite of how unworthy or how unlovely they are to you.[4]

Of course, we can feel that our prodigals are unworthy and undeserving, and that their behavior is surely unlovely. After all, we have endured, waited, encouraged, helped, pleaded, and wept. At some point do we say, "Stop. No more grace!"?

God doesn't.

He extends *unending* grace. He loves us and accepts us and keeps His welcoming arms open to our return.

But what about consequences? What about standards in our home? What about safety for our family? What about requiring responsibility? Yes, those are all needful and appropriate. But grace is still possible.

Swindoll adds:

No one expects you to excuse the sin of the unlovely, nor should you become their doormat. Extending grace doesn't send the message that you approve of their behavior. And don't fall into the trap of fearing that grace enables people in their sin. In fact, grace brings conviction to the heart of the sinner much more quickly than a rebuke.[5]

So how do we extend grace to rebellious, unappreciative prodigals? Perhaps there will be a major opportunity—like a repentant request to return home. But most often it will be in little things we do—an unexpected favor, returning a curse with a blessing, taking them out to dinner, listening to them, sending a note or a text.

When Josh was still a minor living at home and he did something especially aggravating, I would do his laundry for him. Washing his clothes was his responsibility, but I would say, as I put each piece in the washing machine, "I choose to bless you, not curse you." I don't know if he was grateful for that grace, but it did wonders for me!

Bill Bright, founder of Campus Crusade for Christ (now Cru), provided an amazing model for me in giving grace. When a Christian leader would fall because of some act of immorality, much of the body of Christ would criticize, judge, reject, condemn. But Dr. Bright would always be one of the first to call, to pray for, to listen to the leader . . . and to extend grace.

Can we stoop to give grace to our loved ones?

RESPONSE:

1. When are you most tempted to stop giving grace?
2. How might you extend grace to your prodigal when he clearly doesn't deserve it?

DAY 14: The Voice of Grace

"That's disgraceful!"

"You are so ungrateful."

"That behavior makes you *persona non grata* here."

Each of these phrases contains a word with the Latin root for grace—or lack of it. They all mean "without grace." And they are words that any of us might have said to our prodigals, because they have been true.

Yet God tells us just the opposite should be true of the words we speak. They should be full of grace:

- "Your lips have been anointed with grace, since God has blessed you forever" (Psalm 45:2).

- "One who loves a pure heart and who speaks with grace will have the king for a friend" (Proverbs 22:11).
- "May our Lord Jesus Christ himself and God our Father, who loved us and by his grace gave us eternal encouragement and good hope, encourage your hearts and strengthen you in every good deed and word" (2 Thessalonians 2:16–17).
- "Let your conversation be always full of grace, seasoned with salt, so that you may know how to answer everyone" (Colossians 4:6).

I am convinced that one of the most important ways we extend grace to our prodigals is through our words.

Words are powerful. They have either the potential to inflame discord and inflict great emotional harm, or the capacity to encourage repentance and restoration and offer healing and reconciliation.

Certainly we must speak truth, and our prodigals often need to hear some hard truths. But God's Word reminds us *how* we must deliver those words: "Instead, speaking the truth in love, we will in all things grow up into him who is the Head, that is, Christ" (Ephesians 4:15 NIV1984).

Speak it *in love.*

Easy? No. Our frustration prompts negative words. Disrespect from a prodigal elicits a raised voice from us. Anger arouses other emotions. Conflict escalates.

How *do* we speak truth in love? How do we make sure our words are seasoned with grace?

Some practical thoughts:

- Wait: Count to ten before you speak.
- Moderate: Speak slowly, calmly, gently, and firmly.
- Think: Will these words add fuel to the fire?
- Consider: Would you like someone to speak such words in that tone of voice to you?

- Recognize: The words you speak today may be part of your relationship with your prodigal for all the years to come.
- Realize: Your tone of voice can turn neutral words into destructive words.
- Remember: You love this person!
- Pray: Most of all, stop to pray before you speak. Make sure you are filled with God's Spirit. Ask Him to govern your tongue, to release His love into your heart. Choose to be an instrument of God's grace.

Gracious words may or may not lessen the carnage in the immediate "conversation," though they should help. But over time, words filled with grace will eliminate the fuel that feeds what often becomes an inferno. When grace has prevailed and the words we have spoken have not done irreparable harm, then return, reconciliation, and restoration will occur more easily.

Love speaks grace. So should we.

RESPONSE:

1. How have words without grace contributed to an escalating confrontation with your loved one?
2. When have you seen grace-filled words contribute to peace and resolution?

DAY 15: Grace Forgives

Les Misérables by Victor Hugo is a powerful story of forgiveness and redemption. Jean Valjean was a hardened man when he was released from prison after serving nineteen years for stealing bread. Looking for a place to sleep, he was invited in by a kind bishop. In the night, though, Valjean stole silver from the bishop and sneaked away.

The next morning the police brought him to the bishop, silver in hand. The bishop's response, as I recall it: "So there you are. I'm delighted to see you. Had you forgotten that I gave you the candlesticks as well? Did you forget to take them?" And to the police: "This gentleman was no thief. This silver was my gift to him."

That was the beginning of Valjean's transformation.[6]

Reading that story had a powerful impact on my response to our prodigal. It was the beginning of some very dark days of our journey with our son, and, as I mentioned before, God spoke this strong word to me: *"When you make mistakes with this boy"*—and I made many—*"err on the side of grace."*

What? What about the truth of wrong actions and their consequences? Of course there were consequences. What about enabling his poor choices? No, we didn't want to enable.

It takes supernatural wisdom to blend justice based on truth with benevolence based on grace.

But God was clear: Forgive. Extend grace. Seek reconciliation. Pursue conversation, not conflict. Keep your doors—and arms— open. It's not a balancing of truth and grace—it's a *blending* of 100 percent truth and 100 percent grace.

God is our model here. When I want to make sure my prodigal experiences the painful results of his bad choices, I think of how God has responded to *my* many bad choices: Mercy. Forgiveness. Grace.

His Word underlines this repeatedly:

- "For if you forgive other people when they sin against you, your heavenly Father will also forgive you" (Matthew 6:14).
- "If he sins against you seven times in a day, and seven times comes back to you and says, 'I repent,' forgive him" (Luke 17:4 NIV1984).
- "Jesus said, 'Father, forgive them, for they do not know what they are doing'" (Luke 23:34).

Philip Yancey writes:

Like grace, forgiveness has about it the maddening quality of being undeserved, unmerited, unfair. . . .

The gospel of grace begins and ends with forgiveness. . . . Grace is the only force in the universe powerful enough to break the chains that enslave generations. Grace alone melts ungrace.[7]

Henri Nouwen comments on forgiveness:

. . . even as I have said [I forgive you] . . . I still wanted to hear the story that tells me that I was right . . . I still wanted the satisfaction of receiving some praise in return . . . for being so forgiving.

But God's forgiveness is unconditional; it comes from a heart that does not demand anything for itself. . . . It is this divine forgiveness that I have to practice in my daily life. . . . It demands that I step over that wounded part of my heart that feels hurt and wronged and that wants to stay in control and put a few conditions between me and the one whom I am asked to forgive.[8]

And again from Philip Yancey:

. . . forgiveness is an act of faith. By forgiving another, I am trusting that God is a better justice-maker than I am. . . . I leave in God's hands the scales that must balance justice and mercy. . . . Though wrong does not disappear when I forgive, it loses its grip on me and is taken over by God, who knows what to do.[9]

Following is a brief prayer you might pray, expressing your choice to forgive your loved prodigal. You may have to pray it many times—I have.

Father, thank you for your mercy and grace toward me, and for forgiving my sins through Jesus' death on the cross. Thank you that you forgive me over and over, for repeated sins and for new sins, big or small. I am so grateful for your grace.

Lord, I need to forgive _____, my loved one who has wronged me, hurt me, betrayed me, offended me, sinned against me. It is hard for me to do this—I am still hurt, angry, confused. So

I come asking you for the power to forgive _____.
*Fill me with your Spirit and remind me of your love and mercy to
me—and to* _____.

By your Spirit, I choose to forgive _____. *I
choose to extend grace and mercy to him/her, even as you have
done for me. I choose, as you enable me, to live at peace with this
person I love. I ask that you* _____ *in your love.
May we be reconciled and our relationship healed. And if that does
not happen, may I continue to love and forgive.*

*Thank You that this is possible in the power of your Spirit.
In Jesus' name, Amen.*

RESPONSE:

1. What is your response to my assurance that I should "err on
   the side of grace"?
2. How might praying such a prayer of forgiveness bring healing in your relationship with your loved one?

DAY 16: Scandalous Grace

"Not fair!!!"

How many times has your prodigal said that? How many times
have *you* said that? And how often is that our response to the scandalous grace of God? Our Bibles are full of stories of undeserved
grace:

David: Faithful shepherd boy. Courageous defeater of Goliath.
Chosen king of Israel. One who wouldn't raise his hand against
Saul, God's anointed, who was trying to kill him. Conqueror of the
pagan tribes of Palestine. Author of half of the Psalms. And, oh yes,
adulterer and murderer. Yet he was *a man after God's own heart*
(1 Samuel 13:14).

Rahab: Lived in pagan Jericho. Prostitute. Liar. Yes, she saved the Israelites who came to spy on Jericho. But did she really deserve to be in the family tree of David—and of Jesus (Joshua 6:17; Matthew 1:5)?

Saul/Paul: A righteous Pharisee. A defender of Judaism. A Hebrew of Hebrews. But also a persecutor of The Way. Murderer of Christians. By his own words, "the worst of sinners." But Paul is considered the greatest teacher—besides Jesus—of the New Testament (1 Timothy 1:12–16).

How is it possible that God could use such sinners?

Grace. Scandalous grace.

Jesus' actions, as well as His stories, reflected the same "unfairness," the same grace:

The woman at the well: Jews avoided going through Samaria, but Jesus "had to go through Samaria." Why? He had an appointment to keep with a woman of questionable character. Five husbands, and now living with a man not her husband. Jesus knew all this. Yet He talked to her—a Samaritan, a woman, a sinner. He told her what he knew about her, but he didn't condemn. Instead he offered her living water and a changed life (John 4).

The parable of the workers: Some started early morning, others midday, still others at the end of the day. And they all were paid the same—an amount to which they had agreed. What? Unfair! Those who worked one hour were paid the same as those who worked all day? But the landowner asked, "Are you envious because I am generous?" (Matthew 20:15).

The thief on the cross: An evil man, certainly, to have earned crucifixion as punishment for his crimes. Yet even as he is dying, he asks for mercy from Jesus. Jesus could have said, "It's too late. You have lived a terrible life. You are only repenting now because you are afraid." But no, Jesus said, "Today you will be with me in Paradise" (Luke 23:43).

How is it possible that God could look beyond the actions of such people?

Grace. Scandalous grace.

Is it fair that someone who has been a terrible parent has wonderful children, yet you, who have tried to do everything right, have such a prodigal child? Of course not.

Is it fair that your prodigal, who has hurt you repeatedly, abused your kindness, rejected your love, should be forgiven and welcomed back? Of course not.

But is it fair that we, imperfect, inadequate, unworthy as we are, should be forgiven, redeemed, and bound for eternity with our God? Of course not.

You see, we are addicted to fairness, to justice, to revenge, to earning our way, to performance. Yet in reality, we truly don't want God to respond to us based on those addictions.

We can't help but be grateful that God favors grace. Yes, scandalous grace! And He wants to pour out that grace on us, but also through us to those much loved—though hardly lovable—prodigals.

So let's enter into, with whole hearts, God's scandalous grace.

RESPONSE:

1. When has your prodigal said, "Not fair"? When have you said it?

2. How might you give scandalous grace to your loved one?

DAY 17: The Grace-full Father

If you have a prodigal, you surely know this story. It's the story of the Prodigal Son. Some of us have realized it is about two prodigal sons—the repentant younger and the resentful elder. (But for this application, we will stick to the younger.)

And it's really about the Grace-full Father (Luke 15:11–31).

First, a little synopsis, and then some personalization and application.

What the son did: He shamed his father by asking for his inheritance—which is equal to wishing his father to be dead. He took a significant portion of his father's livelihood. He sinned extravagantly—which is the original meaning of *prodigal*. He squandered his inheritance with wild living. Then he despaired, repented, and returned.

What the father did: He gave the son his inheritance. He let him go. He watched and waited (and I imagine prayed). When he saw his son coming, he ran to him, embraced him, kissed him. Then he threw a party for him. He reinstated him into the family. Does this make sense? *No!* Did the son deserve such grace? *No!*

What I have done: I could make a long list of my sins—all the usual ones, generally not the "big" ones. I have sought to follow Him, obey Him, live and love like Jesus. And too often I have failed. I have disobeyed, shamed, dishonored, and abandoned my heavenly Father and have misused His generous gifts.

What my heavenly Father has done: He created me in His image, for definite purposes. He has pursued me, purchased me, redeemed me, reconciled me, forgiven me. He adopted me as His very own loved daughter. He invited me into His presence, talked with me, enjoyed me. He welcomed me back over and over. He extended amazing grace to me. Does this make sense? *No!* Do I deserve such grace? *No!*

What my prodigal has done: He has done many prodigal things: lied, stolen, disrespected us. He's used and abused alcohol, drugs, girls, our home. He went through many cars in a few years. He spent time in a juvenile detention center and in jail. Okay, I'll stop; that covers most of the big things.

My response: I tried to do what we are told we should do: I established boundaries, enforced consequences, helped him to move out. I got counseling—for him and for us. I sought advice, listened, scolded, pleaded, preached. I prayed. And prayed. And prayed. I welcomed him back, encouraged him, homeschooled him. I extended much grace. I have done some things well, other things not well at all. Does he deserve the grace given over and over? *No!* Was I right to give grace? *Yes!*

So now it's your turn: What has your prodigal done? How have you responded? Would grace call for any different response?

RESPONSE:

1. What feelings does the father's response to his returning son arouse in you?
2. What feelings has this exercise prompted in you?

DAY 18: More Than Enough Grace

This story is about a friend and his prodigal son:

We (the Prayer for Prodigals community) have prayed for a young man over the years. He was estranged, then reunited with his dad. He and his girlfriend had a baby. He returned to drugs and alcohol.

One day, high on drugs, he drove erratically down the highway and caused a crash in which a woman was killed. He is now spending many years in prison.

His dad was devastated. "How could this happen?" he asked, heartbroken. "Is there no future for my son?"

But after days and weeks spent on his knees and in the Word, the dad found peace. He writes: "God's majesty shrinks at no one's behavior. Everything we know is for God. He uses every last thread of our lives. How he uses it? We only get to participate, not know exactly his will at any particular time. He's the Lord's first, mine second. I can only be here for him and be still."

God's grace was sufficient for my friend.

God said, "My grace is sufficient for you, for my power is made perfect in weakness" (2 Corinthians 12:9).

God's grace is enough.

We have barely scratched the surface on the height and width and depth of God's grace. I have not intended to be exhaustive on this incomprehensible topic. But there are a few more things I want to mention.

Grace is an undeserved free gift, undeserved favor, and undeserved love. And it is more than enough for any person, circumstance, tragedy, need.

God's grace has made His love and salvation and provision—everything He offers—available to us. But there is a catch. In order to live in it, we must receive it.

He gives us a little understanding of who will be able to truly access and experience that grace: those who are humble. "But he gives us more grace. That is why Scripture says: 'God opposes the proud but gives grace to the humble'" (James 4:6 NIV1984).

This truth is repeated several times, and it is the first step toward accepting God's grace—understanding that you don't deserve it.

But that grace is abundantly sufficient.

We are saved by grace. "For it is by grace you have been saved, through faith—and this not from yourselves, it is the gift of God—not by works, so that no one can boast" (Ephesians 2:8–9).

God freely gives the grace that saves us—we cannot earn salvation. And it is that same freely given grace that will save our prodigals. Keeping the rules, doing the right things, not doing the wrong things—none of this will save us or them.

Only grace is sufficient to save us.

Grace enables good works. "And God is able to bless you abundantly, so that in all things at all times, having all that you need, you will abound in every good work" (2 Corinthians 9:8).

Good works, doing the right thing, not doing the wrong thing—these all matter and are desirable. But we can't live that perfect life ourselves.

Only grace is enough to enable us to live like Jesus.

I remember the day I had first written those words above. On that same day, my son told me of another wrong choice, and my emotions took over. At first I didn't access that grace to speak kindly and to believe the best. Then God reminded me of what I had just been writing: Only grace is enough to enable me to live like Jesus—so I once again received that grace. . . .

And His grace was more than enough.

RESPONSE:

1. How did you respond to the story of the father and his incarcerated son?
2. When have you seen God give more than enough grace to you in your wilderness journey?

3

TIME

I am the LORD. In its time, I will do this swiftly.

Isaiah 60:22

Surely one of the most common questions asked by those who love a prodigal is, "How long, Lord?"

For all of us, time is such a controlling element. We don't have enough time to do everything. We need to manage time and use it well.

As our children grow, we move between "Will this phase ever end?" and "How did they grow up so fast?" When things are difficult or boring, time drags; when life is good, time flies.

But when you love a prodigal, it can seem like time stands still, and you wonder, *Will this never end?*

In this chapter, let's try to enter into God's perspective on time, to rest in His timing, and even to wait with hope and expectancy.

DAY 19: In Its Time

"It's the waiting, isn't it?"

That's what I wrote several years ago in a letter to lovers of prodigals. I continued:

> Will it ever end? Will change ever come? Will the pain, confusion, fear, anger, despair ever end?
>
> During the dozen plus years it took our son to turn from his bad choices, we waited. On our knees. With tears. Clinging to Jesus.
>
> In the past few years, things have been much better. He is not making the terrible choices he did for so long. I don't call him a prodigal now. He has become responsible and hardworking. We have a great relationship. There is trust. But still we wait. . . .

So, did that good time last? What about the year that followed?

It was very challenging. His marriage fell apart. In his despair, he fell into old patterns, making choices of the past. A brief reunion with his wife crashed, and that marriage ended in divorce. He went into deep depression.

And I said, many times, "I thought it was time! Isn't it time, Lord, for change that lasts? Are we doing this again? How long, Lord?"

I know you understand.

We know that God is bigger than time. We know all the truths of Scripture:

> **Moses:** "A thousand years in your sight are like a day that has just gone by, or like a watch in the night" (Psalm 90:4).
>
> **David:** "But I trust in you, LORD; I say, 'You are my God.' My times are in your hands" (Psalm 31:14–15).

Isaiah: "'For my thoughts are not your thoughts, neither are your ways my ways,' declares the LORD" (Isaiah 55:8).

Many times, many days, even many years, we struggle to accept, act on, live by, rest in—believe—these truths. It seems too hard, too long, too uncertain. How long, Lord? Will it ever end?

But these statements are true. They are reality. And that is what we will look at, delve into, and listen for in this chapter: God's perspective on time—for our prodigals, for us, for the kingdom, for eternity.

One verse has especially sustained me over these years: "I am the LORD. In its time, I will do this swiftly" (Isaiah 60:22).

Let's consider, phrase by phrase, what the Lord is saying to us through these words to the children of Israel just before their return from seventy years of captivity.

"I am the LORD." Such a needed reminder for me.

You've seen the sayings "from God"—the variations online, on Facebook, on wall plaques and billboards: "I am God and you are not."

Sure, I have many good ideas, plans, schedules for how things should play out for my life—and for my loved one. But God reminds me who is in control.

"In its time . . ." I so want "its time" to be now, to be "my time." It rarely is.

"I . . ." This "I," of course, is God, not I.

"will do this . . ." We cannot make it happen. But He can and will.

"swiftly." I love that. Soon. Now. No more waiting. But the swiftness is not "in my time" but in "its [God-ordained] time."

As I have been in the Word, asking God what He wants to say to us about time, I have looked at the concepts of days and years, today and tomorrow, and especially the idea of waiting. Oh, how rich were my findings! How great God is—how puny I am. How intentional God is—all in love and with grace.

RESPONSE:

1. In the verse we just took apart, the phrase "its time" seems to imply the particular time needed for this good thing to happen, from God's point of view. How might this perspective give you hope?

2. Which of the other Scriptures shared in this section mean the most to you today? Explain.

DAY 20: Pearls, Butterflies, and Prodigals

What do pearls and butterflies have in common?

They both start out as something simple and not so beautiful and are transformed into something lovely.

A pearl begins as a tiny grain of sand in an oyster. Since—to the oyster—it is an irritant, the oyster immediately begins to cover the grain with nacre, the same substance its shell is made from. Over time, because of the pressure experienced by the oyster, layer after layer of nacre transforms that grain of sand into a lustrous pearl.

Most of us have marveled at how a caterpillar—an ugly, hairy, wormlike creature crawling on a tree limb—can become a lovely butterfly soaring through the sky. Perhaps you have even watched the process as a school science experiment. And you've heard that a butterfly, which has been under pressure while tightly packed in its chrysalis, must go through the difficult effort to break out if it is to be able to fly.

Oh, how we wish our prodigals would return *now*. How we want them to be changed overnight! And sometimes that happens. Amazing surrender and metamorphosis can happen in a moment or a day or a week. But not usually. Usually it takes both time and pressure.

What kind of pressure? Many kinds, actually:

Hurting and disappointing those they love, which matters to them more than they acknowledge or we feel. Choices that lead to negative consequences—from small to very significant. Hunger, pain, exposure, poverty. Loss of identity, community, family. Loss of hope for a good future. All for momentary pleasure or a sense of personal freedom.

And time? It takes time for the pain and reality of those losses and consequences to sink in. It also takes time for most prodigals to recognize they are not really happy with their current situation and to start to look for a better approach to life—to begin to make a turn. Finally, even when the decision to turn is real, it takes time for consequences to play out, for addictions to be overcome, for habits and patterns to reverse.

Transformation requires both time and pressure.

Sometimes we grow weary under the stress and the seemingly endless pain. "Now, please, Lord."

But our God has given us this word: "He has made everything beautiful in its time" (Ecclesiastes 3:11).

So just as it takes time to transform a grain of sand into an exquisite pearl, and to change a caterpillar into a lovely butterfly, so it will take time for our loved ones to be transformed into the beautiful ones God created them to be.

And each of us also needs transforming, in small and large places in our lives. That change will also require time and pressure. And in God's economy, surely our prodigal loved ones are supplying time and pressure in great amounts, yielding newness in our lives as well. God is a good steward and He also has a sense of humor.

RESPONSE:

1. What beautiful things have you seen God bring into your life?
2. Which have been the result of time and pressure?

DAY 21: At the Very Time God Promised

For many years, every time my birthday would come around, I'd tell my son what gift I would like from him. It was always the same gift.

"All I want for my birthday is for you to surrender your life to Jesus."

There were times he yelled at me in response: "I want nothing to do with Jesus!"

Other times he didn't acknowledge my request—not a no, not a yes, just silence.

Often he would make small steps toward surrendering to God, giving me little tokens of hope. But still I waited for that very special gift.

Abraham and Sarah also waited many years for a very special gift—the birth of their son, Isaac.

There was a promise: "Then the word of the LORD came to him: 'This man will not be your heir, but a son who is your own flesh and blood will be your heir.' He took him outside and said, 'Look up at the sky and count the stars—if indeed you can count them.' Then he said to him, 'So shall your offspring be'" (Genesis 15:4–5).

There was a bypass: "Now Sarai, Abram's wife, had borne him no children. But she had an Egyptian slave named Hagar; so she said to Abram, 'The LORD has kept me from having children. Go, sleep with my slave; perhaps I can build a family through her'" (Genesis 16:1–2).

There was an affirmation: "Is anything too hard for the LORD? I will return to you at the appointed time next year, and Sarah will have a son" (Genesis 18:14).

Then there was the fulfillment: "Sarah became pregnant and bore a son to Abraham in his old age, at the very time God had promised him" (Genesis 21:2).

Abraham had a promise: His descendants would outnumber the stars in the sky. Yet he had no child, no heir, no tangible evidence of God's promise. Year after year, he looked for the promise. Time after time, the impossible did not happen.

Been there. Waiting for the birthday gift.

Sarai couldn't wait. She took things into her own hands, trying to come up with her own solution.

Uh oh! Been there too. No, I couldn't make him say, "I surrender." But a little manipulation, maybe a small bribe, some demanding prayers: "Do it my way, God."

I take such encouragement in God's creativity. Yes, pain and disruption and conflict resulted from Sarai's effort—then and to this day. Yet God redeemed it; He protected Hagar and Ishmael throughout their lives. And in Genesis 16:13–14, Hagar gave us a beautiful understanding with this name of God: *El Roi*—"the God who sees me."

I would wonder if Abram and Sarai's efforts (he *did* participate!) wouldn't have caused God himself to take a bypass as well, to go with another approach. But no, God reaffirmed the original plan: Abraham at ninety-nine and Sarah at ninety would have a son in a year. And it happened. Exactly when God planned it to happen. Talk about a birth-day celebration! I suppose Isaac is the longest-waited-for baby ever.

I've had promises about my son. Maybe you, too, have had promises about your loved ones. Or maybe you wait and despair and pray and hope. Repeat. Repeat. Will the time ever come?

God is not bound by time, but He operates in time. And He reminds us: He will accomplish His purposes in the lives of our prodigals—children, spouses, parents, friends—in His perfect way at His perfect time. And He will do the same in our own lives.

RESPONSE:

1. Have you, like Sarai, tried to take things into your own hands? How did it play out?
2. When have you seen God graciously redeem your own efforts, your own "bypasses"?

DAY 22: The Enemy Looks for the Right Time

One of the hardest parts of the wilderness journey with a loved prodigal is the roller coaster—the ups and downs, the unexpected turns, the dashed hope.

I know. I lived it. My loved one was making great progress. Better choices. Greater stability. Hope for a good future.

Then hard things happened, pain seared, despair overcame. Bad choices ensued. Old patterns returned. I felt like we had reverted to ten years earlier.

Why was I surprised?

We have an enemy. That enemy is after those we love: "Be alert and of sober mind. Your enemy the devil prowls around like a roaring lion looking for someone to devour" (1 Peter 5:8). And, "The thief comes only to steal and kill and destroy" (John 10:10).

He is wily and smart. He studies your prodigal and my prodigal—to know the right temptation, the stumbling block most likely to succeed, the best time to attack.

Again, why should we be surprised? He did it to our Lord (Luke 4:1–12).

When the enemy followed Jesus into the wilderness, he was intent on destruction. But he was clever. He waited until he thought Jesus would be weak from hunger and thirst. He used the Father's own words—quoting Scripture repeatedly. He offered Jesus shortcuts—an easier way—to what was already to be His: power, authority, immortality.

Jesus, of course, was not deceived. He saw through the devil's schemes. He used Scripture to rebuke the devil, to resist him, to say, "No!"

"When the devil had finished all this tempting, he left him until *an opportune time*" (Luke 4:13, emphasis added).

Satan is such an opportunist.

He is ever vigilant to recapture our loved ones, to regain the advantage, to remind them of the pleasures of sin, to woo them back into places they have left. He watches for an opportune time.

We have some clear instructions: "Submit yourselves, then, to God. Resist the devil, and he will flee from you" (James 4:7).

We can pray that our prodigals will remember the teaching they have received and resist the devil themselves. But often they will not be at a place in their lives to do that.

So we must stand in the gap. I did that for three nights after our son received Christ (See "Love Goes to War" in chapter 1, "Love."), and I have been doing so since. If you are praying for a prodigal, you know how you must pray.

We must pray on their behalf. We ask God to be their strong fortress, to protect them, to strengthen them, to point them to His way of escape from temptation (1 Corinthians 10:13). We must take the offensive against the evil one, according to scriptural patterns. (For more about spiritual warfare, see the references for this chapter as well as "Battlefront Prayer" in chapter 6, "Prayer.")

We must personally make sure we are resisting the devil and his temptations directed at us. We must walk with Christ in humility and holiness and in the power of the Spirit. All that we ask God to do on behalf of our prodigals we must ask Him to do for us.

"Finally, be strong in the Lord and in his mighty power. Put on the full armor of God, so that you can take your stand against the devil's schemes" (Ephesians 6:10–11).

RESPONSE:

1. When have you realized that the enemy was using the stumbling block most likely to succeed against you?

2. How does that help you to understand your prodigal's vulnerability to the same enemy?

DAY 23: Weary in the Waiting

Weary.

Weary for the pain. The surprises. The expense. The disappointment. The late-night calls. The fear.

Weary in the waiting.

Sometimes it is challenging to follow through with this exhortation: "Let us not become weary in doing good, for at the proper time we will reap a harvest if we do not give up" (Galatians 6:9).

Doing good? Are we? Surely the loving, the disciplining, the grace-giving, the exhorting, the praying are good. Yet sometimes the good changes—the hoped-for, prayed-for, begged-for changes—never seem to come.

But wait. Is there good in the waiting? God seems to say so. Let these many words on waiting sink in:

- "LORD, I wait for you; you will answer, Lord my God" (Psalm 38:15).
- "But if we hope for what we do not yet have, we wait for it patiently" (Romans 8:25).
- "For the creation waits in eager expectation for the children of God to be revealed" (Romans 8:19).
- "Wait for the LORD; be strong and take heart and wait for the LORD" (Psalm 27:14).

- "In the morning, LORD, you hear my voice; in the morning I lay my requests before you and wait expectantly" (Psalm 5:3).
- "Be patient, then, brothers and sisters, until the Lord's coming. See how the farmer waits for the land to yield its valuable crop, patiently waiting for the autumn and spring rains" (James 5:7).
- "I waited patiently for the LORD; he turned to me and heard my cry" (Psalm 40:1).
- "I wait for the LORD, my whole being waits, and in his word I put my hope" (Psalm 130:5).
- "Since ancient times no one has heard, no ear has perceived, no eye has seen any God besides you, who acts on behalf of those who wait for him" (Isaiah 64:4).
- "For the revelation awaits an appointed time; it speaks of the end and will not prove false. Though it linger, wait for it; it will certainly come and will not delay" (Habakkuk 2:3).

Think of those people throughout Scripture who waited: Abraham for a child; Joseph to get out of prison; Moses for Pharaoh to let his people go; the children of Israel in the desert to reach the Promised Land; Simeon and Anna the prophetess to see Jesus; the disciples for the Holy Spirit. Think of those who waited for rain, for a word from God, or for the Messiah.

And God waits too.

He has waited through all the prodigalness of His children. He waited for just the right time to send His Son in the incarnation, and now waits for the right time to send Him again. And He waits for each of us and each of our loved ones to surrender, to accept, to return, to trust. . . .

So we wait.

"Yet the LORD longs to be gracious to you; therefore he will rise up to show you compassion. For the LORD is a God of justice. Blessed are all who wait for him!" (Isaiah 30:18).

RESPONSE:

1. Have you begun to recognize the good in waiting? If not, what might be keeping you from embracing this idea?
2. How has it helped you to know that God himself waits?

DAY 24: Always and Never

You are aware of the reality of *always* and *never*.

We know that when we say our loved one "always" does something, or our prodigal says we "always" say some specific thing, it just isn't true. People are never that consistent—no one *always* does or says the same thing.

Then there's the "never" jinx: If that prodigal or we ourselves say to God that we will never do something, there is a high probability we will eventually do just that.

And communication and counseling advice is that we should not use *never* or *always* in working through relationships.

But God seems to love these words! They specifically mean "all the time" and "at no time." He has some "always" and "never" instructions for us, and some promises to us, that include those words. Here are just a few.

Admonitions and Encouragement for Us

"[Love] always protects, always trusts, always hopes, always perseveres" (1 Corinthians 13:7). We love our prodigals, don't we! It's a strong, deep love that gives so much and puts up with so much. Yet God calls us to some challenging "all-the-times": always protect, always trust, always hope, always persevere. Clearly that kind of love must be given to us by God himself.

"And as for you, brothers and sisters, never tire of doing what is good" (2 Thessalonians 3:13). Over and over, as we live with and love our prodigals, we get to choose to do good to them, to do the right thing, to model what "good" looks like. How weary we become. Yet our Father, who is doing the same for us day after day, year after year, says, "Never tire of doing what is good." He shows us how it's done, and He fills us with His Spirit to give us the power to follow His pattern and keep doing good too.

"We always thank God, the Father of our Lord Jesus Christ, when we pray for you" (Colossians 1:3). Of course, we pray for them. We beg, we plead, we cry. But do we say "Thank you"? God reminds us that our prayers for our prodigals should always include thanksgiving to Him. Thanks for what? For His goodness and faithfulness, for our very-much-loved one, for the challenges and pain he or she causes us, for God's good work in them and in us—even if we can't always see it.

Promises and Assurances from God

"And surely I am with you always, to the very end of the age" (Matthew 28:20). Just before He departed the earth, the Lord Jesus promised His disciples—and us—that He would always be with them, with us. We are never alone in this wilderness journey. I think of His leading the way, guarding behind me, and walking beside me.

"God has said, 'Never will I leave you; never will I forsake you'" (Hebrews 13:5). Just in case we didn't really believe that He is always with us, He gives us this powerful assurance. I especially love it in the Amplified version: "[God] has said, 'I will never [under any circumstances] desert you [nor give you up nor leave you without support, nor will I in any degree leave you helpless], nor will I forsake or let you down or relax My hold on you [assuredly not]!'" (Hebrews 13:5 AMP). Wow!

"I give them eternal life, and they shall never perish; no one will snatch them out of my hand" (John 10:28). I love this promise. If our prodigals have become children of God at some time, though now they deny Him or walk away from Him, Jesus says He gives them eternal life and they shall never perish. Thank You, Lord. And as I see the constant attacks and pursuits of the evil one, how I claim that assurance that no one will be able to snatch them out of the hand of Jesus.

". . . because he always lives to intercede for them" (Hebrews 7:25). We pray. Oh, how we pray. But sometimes I don't know what to pray. Too often I feel like my prayers accomplish nothing. Then I remember: Jesus always lives to intercede for them. I am so grateful.

So I encourage you to *always* believe and *never* give up.

RESPONSE:

1. What "always" or "never" statements have you or your prodigal said to each other?
2. Which always/never words from God do you appreciate the most today? Explain.

DAY 25: God Is Always at Work

"He's building his testimony."

My friend Diane has been a faithful prayer warrior on behalf of our son. I used to pass her on the way to my office, and she always asked how he was doing. On the days there were more bad choices, more reasons to despair, she often responded, "He's building his testimony."

With those words, God kept reminding me of this important truth from Jesus: "My Father is always at his work to this very day, and I too am working" (John 5:17).

When our loved one is doing destructive things—whether from childish thinking, lack of thinking, gratifying the flesh, evil intent, or from just being foolish—our tendency is often to sigh or cry or despair. Yet God is at work even in all this. He is at work in our prodigals, He is at work in these circumstances, and He is at work in us.

One of my favorite verses assures me that God was intentional when He made each of us—including our loved ones—designing us perfectly for the plans He has created for us: "For we are God's handiwork, created in Christ Jesus to do good works, which God prepared in advance for us to do" (Ephesians 2:10).

The word *workmanship* has been translated "handiwork, work of art, masterpiece"!

And how often I take comfort in this promise, for myself and for my prodigal: "Being confident of this, that he who began a good work in you will carry it on to completion until the day of Christ Jesus" (Philippians 1:6).

I find myself agreeing wholeheartedly with David the psalmist: "The LORD will accomplish what concerns me; Your lovingkindness, O LORD, is everlasting: Do not forsake the works of Your hands" (Psalm 138:8 NASB).

God will use choices—even poor ones—and circumstances to accomplish what He began in each of us, building a testimony for future good works.

Moses said the same thing to the Israelites at the Red Sea: "Do not fear! Stand by and see the salvation of the LORD which He will accomplish for you today" (Exodus 14:13 NASB).

Job, just before the end of his ordeal, understood: "I know that You can do all things, and that no purpose of Yours can be thwarted" (Job 42:2 NASB).

Not long ago, I reread *Hinds' Feet on High Places*, the story of little Much-Afraid and her journey to the high places to live with the Good Shepherd. During a particularly difficult time, when Much-Afraid spent her days making her way through a dense fog, she despaired that the Shepherd had abandoned her and she felt she would never find her way. But when the Shepherd came to her and she asked Him why she was lost in the fog, He replied, "I am working in ways you cannot see."[1]

Oh, how true that is for us as we live in the fog of our prodigal's delinquency.

How many times have you held on to this next promise? "And we know that in all things God works for the good of those who love him, who have been called according to his purpose" (Romans 8:28).

Finally, from my favorite prophet, Isaiah: "Declaring the end from the beginning, and from ancient times things which have not been done, saying, 'My purpose will be established, and I will accomplish all My good pleasure'" (Isaiah 46:10 NASB).

In other words, God knew what He was doing when He created your loved one, He knows what He is doing now, and He is continuing to work to accomplish His good purposes in and through that life.

Yes, and in our own lives as well.

RESPONSE:

1. How have you seen God at work in you, building your testimony?

2. When has God worked in ways you could not see at the time, but later realized what He had been doing? How does that experience give you hope for your prodigal?

DAY 26: You're in Big Trouble

In this world you will have trouble.
John 16:33

That is not one of my favorite statements from Jesus.

But we know it's true. Everyone will have trouble in this world. For some, it is mostly inconvenient, or a little uncomfortable. For others, it consumes their entire lives—just trying to exist and provide for their basic needs.

For some it is health concerns, for others financial woes, difficult relationships, hard losses. . . .

For those of us who love a prodigal, our troubles seem to revolve around that loved one who seems to choose trouble—and share it with us. And sometimes those troubles last a long time.

God has a lot to say about trouble.

He says to bring Him all that trouble: "Trust in him at all times, you people; pour out your hearts to him, for God is our refuge" (Psalm 62:8).

He offers a safe place in the time of trouble: "The LORD is a refuge for the oppressed, a stronghold in times of trouble" (Psalm 9:9).

He takes care of us when there is trouble: "The LORD is good, a refuge in times of trouble. He cares for those who trust in him" (Nahum 1:7).

Jesus tells us not to worry: "Therefore do not worry about tomorrow, for tomorrow will worry about itself. Each day has enough trouble of its own" (Matthew 6:34).

And then He finishes what He started: "In this world you will have trouble. But take heart! I have overcome the world" (John 16:33).

Overcoming the world? Yes. Even peace in the midst of trouble: "I have told you these things, so that in me you may have peace" (John 16:33).

When I first wrote this section, I was getting to practice Jesus' way of facing trouble. Things with our son were getting better. Communication seemed open and—hopefully—honest. His choices were not catastrophic. But finances were still inadequate, the future was uncertain, and God was not a priority for him. And that particular day was especially troubling.

I poured out my heart to God. I nestled down into that safe refuge. I intentionally handed these troubles to Him. I *chose* to not worry about outcomes.

I kept trusting that His peace would be stronger than any troubles. Well, at least most of the time I was trusting! It didn't help that my son dropped his phone in the ocean that day, and there were no answers, no responses to a couple of questions that I posed to him. Peace was a little spotty, but it came.

"Peace I leave with you; my peace I give you. I do not give to you as the world gives. Do not let your hearts be troubled and do not be afraid" (John 14:27).

RESPONSE:

1. What does it look like when your troubles seem to revolve around your loved one, the one who seems to choose trouble?

2. How are you learning that God truly is your safe refuge and stronghold, where you can nestle down, even during times of trouble?

DAY 27: Now and Forever

Let's go back to the beginning—that is, the beginning of this chapter, or the beginning of your waiting with your loved one, or the beginning of time.

For, of course, with God there is no beginning or ending:

He is the Great I AM: "God said to Moses, 'I AM WHO I AM'" (Exodus 3:14).

He is before and after: "'I am the Alpha and the Omega,' says the Lord God, 'who is, and who was, and who is to come, the Almighty'" (Revelation 1:8).

As we struggle with time, with waiting, with the seemingly endless pain, with giving up hope (which is for the future), it is good to remember that, though God created time, He does not live in time.

He lives in eternity, and He lives in the present, in the now. Again, His name is "I AM." That's present tense. And He calls *us* to live in the present, which is where we find Him.

When we dwell in the past, we relive fear, uncertainty, failure, pain. Or if the past held better times, we hold on to them, wishing they would return.

If we dwell in the future, we dream, we project, we hope, which are not bad things. But we can't know the future, or control it.

God calls us to live in the present, which is all that we really have. He is there with us: "I am with you always" (Matthew 28:20).

And God assures us through David that our times are in His hands (Psalm 31:15).

That's true for those of us who love prodigals, and it is true for those we love. Their times are in His hands, and we can rest in that.

And we can keep praying. For though we live in the present time, *our prayers live in eternity.*

Mark Batterson (author of *The Circle Maker*,[2] a book on prayer) writes in his book *Draw the Circle*:

> Our prayers never die! When we pray, our prayers exit our four dimensions of space-time. Our prayers have no space or time limitations because the God who answers them exists outside of the four dimensions He created. You never know when His timeless answer will reenter the atmosphere of our lives, and that should fill us with holy anticipation. Never underestimate His ability to answer anytime, anyplace, anyhow. He has infinite answers to our finite prayers.[3]

Batterson goes on to recount stories from his own life and others' lives of prayers answered years—even decades—later, sometimes well after the passing of the prayer warrior.

Our God hears our prayers. He treasures them: "Your prayers . . . have come up as a memorial offering before God" (Acts 10:4).

And our God answers our prayers: "In its time I will do this swiftly" (Isaiah 60:22).

We can hold on to this promise from our God who is before and after time, but who dwells with us in the present: "And God is able to bless you abundantly, so that in all things at all times, having all that you need, you will abound in every good work" (2 Corinthians 9:8).

Take courage from David's words on waiting with hope: "I remain confident of this: I will see the goodness of the LORD in the land of the living. Wait for the LORD; be strong and take heart and wait for the LORD" (Psalm 27:13–14).

Because I know who God is and what He is like, and because I understand that He operates in time even though He lives beyond time, I can wait and hope.

I can, in my heart, bind together the difficult present with a hopeful future (in this world) of God's involvement and goodness. I can live in the light of God. I will eagerly anticipate what He will do. I will wait with hope.

RESPONSE:

1. Which is the greater temptation for you: to live in the past with "should have" and "if only," or to live in the future with "how long?" and "what if?"

2. What can you tell yourself right now to help keep your focus on the present?

4

REST

Stand at the crossroads and look;
ask for the ancient paths,
ask where the good way is, and walk in it,
and you will find rest for your souls.
Jeremiah 6:16

Are you tired? Weary? Need a break?

When you love a prodigal, it is usually normal to say "yes!" to those questions.

Our minds are exhausted from striving to know where our prodigals are and what they are doing, and trying to find something that works to bring them back. Our hearts are so weary from the battle, the confusion, the loss, the fear. Even our bodies are tired—depleted from conflict, sleep-deprived, worn out from going to and fro looking for help.

God says, "Take the day off."

He is a fan of rest! He rested after creating the universe. He provided a day of rest for us. In fact, He *commanded* us to rest; He said everyone in the home—plus the animals in their stalls—needs to take a day off and *rest*! He required that even the *land* get a year off every seven years.

I think God is serious about rest. And rest is especially relevant to anyone who loves a prodigal.

In this chapter, our first focus will be on finding rest for ourselves—for our bodies, our minds, and our spirits.

But we will also talk about praying rest for our prodigals. Just think how weary they must be as they fight against us, against their demons and addictions, and against the eternal God. Perhaps some rest for their souls will give them the will to abandon the fight they have chosen and walk a different path.

As the Scripture at the beginning of this chapter encourages, let's look for God's good and ancient paths that wind their way to rest for our souls.

DAY 28: Rest in His Presence

During the darkest years of our journey with our prodigal, I had a friend who was there for me. She came when I needed her. She listened, she wept, she encouraged, she prayed. I could be sure that I could lean against her when I was weak, that she would catch me before I fell, and that she would pick me up when I crashed.

Her presence was often a place of rest for me in the midst of the seemingly never-ending turmoil and weariness. But she could only hold me up for so long. She grew weary in the battle as well.

But there is one who is *always* there for me, who knows and feels my deepest pain, who listens and weeps and encourages and even prays. He invites me to lean on Him. His everlasting arms are always waiting to catch me, and His right hand reaches out to pull me up.

Trying to live away from God's presence is exhausting. We know it. When we try to control our prodigals, we grow weary. Exhaustion haunts us as we pursue every effort to rescue our loved ones.

Our prodigals also grow weary as they run from God and seek pleasure and even meaning for their lives apart from Him.

There is rest in His presence. He says to you and to me, as He said to Moses, "My Presence will go with you, and I will give you rest" (Exodus 33:14).

The psalmist assures, "You make known to me the path of life; you will fill me with joy in your presence, with eternal pleasures at your right hand" (Psalm 16:11).

Jesus himself reminds us, "I am with you always" (Matthew 28:20).

He is always available, waiting for us to come to Him. When we seek Him out, when we dwell in His presence, we will find rest.

The same is true for our prodigals. We can pray for the presence of God to surround them, comfort them, overwhelm them. We can ask God to give them a taste of the rest they are missing as they wander far from His presence.

The apostle John confirms that "we set our hearts at rest in his presence" (1 John 3:19).

RESPONSE:

1. When have you finally given up and fallen into God's arms and the rest He gives?
2. What has helped you to dwell in His presence?

DAY 29: Rest in Repentance

Sin is exhausting. Yes, your prodigal is probably exhausted from all of his or her sinning. But right now, I'm talking about my sin and your sin.

As we struggle through this journey, almost anyone would grant us grace for occasionally raising our voices, responding in anger, saying stupid things, making wussy decisions, or coming down too hard.

Sometimes we sin in those responses, which can weary us. And yes, God gives grace.

Other potential sins go deeper:

Fear. Fear for the safety, future, and life of our loved one. Fear that nothing we try will work and our prodigal will never change. Fear that we will have to live with this pain for the rest of our lives.

Anger. Anger at her for making these terrible choices and not thinking. Anger at ourselves for not doing a better job of influencing, teaching, loving. Anger at God for letting this happen to us.

Not trusting God. How can I believe He is in control? That He loves my prodigal and me when He allows all this pain? That He can bring any good from this mess?

God says it is sin when we continue to live this way—with fear, anger, or distrust—day after day, and this sin will truly exhaust us. It will drain the energy right out of us.

But God also says we don't *have* to live this way. David wrote in Psalm 32 some wonderful words of hope and rest:

> Blessed is the one
>> whose transgressions are forgiven,
>> whose sins are covered.
> Blessed is the one
>> whose sin the Lord does not count against them
>> and in whose spirit is no deceit.
> When I kept silent,
>> my bones wasted away
>> through my groaning all day long.
> For day and night
>> your hand was heavy on me;
> my strength was sapped
>> as in the heat of summer.
> Then I acknowledged my sin to you
>> and did not cover up my iniquity.
> I said, "I will confess
>> my transgressions to the Lord."
> And you forgave the guilt of my sin.
>
> Psalm 32:1–5

There is rest in repentance. God says, "In repentance and rest is your salvation, in quietness and trust is your strength" (Isaiah 30:15).

I love to meditate on Psalms 32 and 51. God speaks to my heart and points out any sin I need to deal with. Then I repent and receive not only mercy and forgiveness, but *rest*. I encourage you to do the same.

Then pray the same things for your prodigal. Your loved one's sins may be different—more blatant—but they are equally exhausting. The possibility of your prodigal returning to his or her senses, to you, and most important, to God, is much better when your loved one finds rest.

RESPONSE:

1. When have you experienced the release and rest that come from not keeping silent, but confessing your failures to your God?

2. As you meditated on Psalms 32 and 51, what lines and phrases were especially relevant to your own current need for rest?

DAY 30: Rest in Forgiveness

I still remember the night he lied to me on his way to spend the night with his girlfriend.

The terrible things he said to me in his drunkenness.

The night he and his drunk friends frightened our houseguest into her room.

And when he stole from his sister.

The lies, the drinking and drugs, the stealing—they happened a lot. There were consequences, but there were also God-enabled grace and mercy.

But those specific events—they have been harder. I have forgiven them many times. I put them behind me and move on in peace. But then something triggers a memory, the pain resurfaces, and the anger returns. And once again I need to consciously extend mercy. I need to forgive. He, of course, knows nothing of this ongoing battle over past pains.

Unforgiveness is exhausting. I'm sure our prodigals will need to know they are forgiven for all they have done—though usually that need comes after they have made some kind of turnaround.

We are the ones who are being worn out and worn down when we are not able to forgive.

Consequences are appropriate. But we also must forgive them—and in forgiveness we will find rest.

By definition, conflict implies lack of rest. Conflict, being wronged, the ongoing battle—all of these bring offense, something we hold on to, and grievances we embrace. And that grasping will surely exhaust us.

There is rest in forgiveness. Jesus has given us the key:

Bear with each other and forgive one another if any of you has a grievance against someone. Forgive as the Lord forgave you.

Colossians 3:13

Blessed are the merciful, for they will be shown mercy.

Matthew 5:7

In essence, He says to us: Forgive and you will be forgiven; show mercy and you will receive mercy.

So is there something you are holding on to, a wrong by your loved one that you have not forgiven? Take it to Jesus. Consciously forgive. Then the door is open for peace. For conflict to dissipate. For *rest*.

RESPONSE:

1. If you are weary, might some of your exhaustion stem from unforgiveness? How will you go about finding and dealing with whatever past pain you may still be clutching?
2. If you are not yet ready to forgive some things your prodigal has done, could you start with forgiving a lesser offense?

DAY 31: Rest in Release

You probably know the story of the monkey who wanted the banana in the bottom of the jar. He thrust his hand right in there and grabbed it—and tried to pull it out. It was stuck. He pulled and pulled, but could not get his hand, which was holding on to that banana, out of that jar.

Until he let go of the fruit.

I tell it another way. When I hold on to something I want, I make a fist to the Lord. Not only does that speak defiance to Him, but it also effectively closes up the opportunity for Him to work in me.

He would have to pry open every finger—to remove what shouldn't be there and/or to put in my hand what He wants to give me.

Oh, how those of us who love prodigals need to hear this. How we hold on to our loved ones, and to our desires for their lives. We plead with them and with God to do what we want. We want to be in control. We manipulate, coerce, bribe—we will do almost anything to make our loved ones come to their senses. Except let go.

Holding on is exhausting. And Jesus offers us an amazing exchange: His perfect way for our imperfect way.

When we willingly (though sometimes reluctantly) open our hands, we give God permission to do His very good work in our lives—and in the lives of our prodigals.

There is rest in release. Below is a declaration of release that I have said many times in God's presence, because I have often taken my prodigal back and needed to release him again.

During your times of prayer, say this declaration of release (a slightly modified version of Sylvia Gunter's in *For the Family*) as often as necessary:

To my loved prodigal:
Because Jesus Christ is my Lord, I free you from my anxiety,
fears, and control. I trust the Holy Spirit to lead you and show

you the way that is right for you—the way of love, joy, and peace, and all that salvation includes.

I place you at God's throne of grace. I cannot force my will on you. I cannot live your life for you. I give you to God the Father, Son, and Holy Spirit. You are a very special person. As much as I love you, God loves you more. Your life today is totally in His hands, and I trust Him with it.

In Jesus' name . . .
I release you from my expectations,
I place you on open palms to the Lord,
I give you my blessings,
I let you go.
In His love,

Date _____

_____ *(signature)*[1]

RESPONSE:

1. Have you ever realized you were making a fist to the Lord? Explain.

2. How might the declaration of release at the end of this section help you defeat the tendency to "take back" and "hold on"?

DAY 32: Rest in Giving Thanks

Why? Why, God?

Why is my loved one making all these terrible choices? Breaking my heart like this?

Why don't you do something, God? Why am I having to go through so much hurt and loss?

These kinds of questions are natural responses to loving a prodigal. Why is this happening to me? Why doesn't God *do* something?

Fighting against reality is exhausting. God calls us instead to a supernatural response: to give thanks "in all circumstances; for this is God's will for you in Christ Jesus" (1 Thessalonians 5:18).

It is God's will for us to give thanks, even in hard times.

Why would I thank God while I am enduring all this pain?

I can think of three wonderful things that happen when I say, "Thank you, Lord":

My focus changes. Instead of fixating on everything I hate about the reality of loving a prodigal, I begin to focus on God and on what He might be doing in this situation.

My trust expands. Just saying "Thank you, Lord" implies "I trust you, God. I believe you are truly God, and that you are truly good." Each time I say it, I believe it more.

Doors open. Saying "Thank you, Lord" is like turning a key that opens locked doors—doors we have bolted shut by demanding that God do things our way. The thank-you key unlatches the bolt and gives God permission to do what He knows is best—in His amazing ability to bring good from really bad.

There is rest in giving thanks. Sometimes giving thanks is really difficult. I found that if I can't yet say "thank you" in the midst of the latest thing my prodigal has done, it helps to think of something I *can* say "thank you" for. Then another. Or if even that is too much of a stretch, I go back to something really big that I am thankful for: Christ's death on the cross for me.

As I began to cultivate the choice to give thanks in every circumstance, the rest and freedom grew in astounding ways.

Say "Thank you, Lord" and get some rest.

RESPONSE:

1. What is your honest reaction to the directive to thank God in every circumstance?
2. If you have started to practice giving thanks even in hard situations, how have you seen your focus changed, your trust expanded, and new doors opened?

DAY 33: Rest on the Right Road

When our prodigal, Josh, was fifteen and in one of his better seasons as a prodigal, he served for a week as a junior counselor at a wilderness camp for at-risk boys. One activity included a five-mile hike, with each counselor leading a small group.

Josh and his boys came to a crossroads, looking for the right turn to take. Unfortunately, they took the wrong turn, and their five-mile hike turned into ten miles. When they finally limped back into camp, they were sore, tired, and unhappy.

Traveling the wrong road is exhausting.

Remember our overarching verse at the beginning of this chapter? It tells us the same thing: "This is what the LORD says: 'Stand at the crossroads and look; ask for the ancient paths, ask where the good way is, and walk in it, and you will find rest for your souls. But you said, "We will not walk in it"'" (Jeremiah 6:16).

Though Josh and his boys didn't intend to choose the wrong path, they did . . . with significant consequences.

Some of our loved ones have not intentionally chosen the wrong path, while others have willfully gone the wrong direction. Either way, they are experiencing the consequences of being on the wrong route.

So our prayer for ourselves and our prodigals is that we and they will choose the right path.

We ask God to open our prodigals' eyes and hearts to His love and goodness so they will want to choose the right way.

We pray that He will create big, thorny hedges to keep them in, and evil out.

We plead for people and circumstances that will steer them away from destructive paths and onto the way of righteousness.

We beg God to allow necessary consequences to show them the emptiness of the direction they are pursuing, but not to let them be destroyed in the process.

These and many other prayers for our prodigals are appropriate and right, and hopeful for their future.

And we should also be praying them for ourselves.

There is rest on the right road.

RESPONSE:

1. From your own experience, why is staying on the right path more restful?

2. What could you pray for your prodigal to help steer her or him in the right direction?

DAY 34: Rest in Obedience

Remember the story I told in the introduction about our adopting Josh? When the child services representative first asked my husband and me if we wanted to adopt him, memories flashed through my mind of a word from God years before: *"I'm sending you a son, and you don't need to do anything about it."*

I thought of how God had brought this boy to us as a nine-year-old foster child, how we sought to love him and care for him, and in return we got ingratitude, disrespect, lies, stealing, trouble at school. . . . Our peaceful home had become chaotic.

So, emotionally, we—my husband and I and our daughters—felt the answer might be no. Why would we sign up for more of the past three years, for permanent chaos?

But God's word came clearly: "I told you I was sending you a son. Why are you rejecting my gift?"

Disobeying a trustworthy God is exhausting.

So we said yes. And in that yes there was rest.

Jesus assures us of that rest in the very presence of God: "Jesus replied, 'Anyone who loves me will obey my teaching. My Father will love them, and we will come to them and make our home with them'" (John 14:23).

In God's instructions to the children of Israel, we learn that our obedience pleases God. "Be careful to obey all these regulations I am giving you, so that it may always go well with you and your children after you, because you will be doing what is good and right in the eyes of the LORD your God" (Deuteronomy 12:28).

We can rest in that affirmation.

See what the writer of Hebrews tells us:

> Therefore, since the promise of entering his rest still stands, let us be careful that none of you be found to have fallen short of it. For we also have had the good news proclaimed to us, just as they did; but the message they heard was of no value to them, because they did not share the faith of those who obeyed. Now we who have believed enter that rest. . . .
>
> Therefore, since it still remains for some to enter that rest, and since those who formerly had the good news proclaimed to them did not go in because of their disobedience, God again set a certain day, calling it "Today." . . .
>
> "Today, if you hear his voice,
> do not harden your hearts." . . .
>
> Let us, therefore, make every effort to enter that rest, so that no one will perish by following their example of disobedience.
>
> Hebrews 4:1–3, 6–7, 11

Here's the really good result: One of the things we desire for our prodigals is to learn obedience. Yes, obedience to us, but especially obedience to God. How will they learn that? By watching *us* walk in obedience.

There is rest in obedience.

RESPONSE:

1. How has disobedience toward God been exhausting in your own life?
2. When have you experienced rest overtaking and enfolding you because you chose to obey God?

DAY 35: Rest in Persevering

We said yes. We adopted him. And there was rest in that obedience.

Hope came: Surely now that he had the security of truly being a part of our family, he would believe we loved him. Perhaps he would connect with us, settle down, experience peace.

Then, despair: Middle school was a wilderness. Teachers couldn't teach with him in the room, so he spent most of his time in alternative classrooms. He caused disruptions on the school bus, so he was banned. He was older and bigger than his classmates, giving him bully status. He joined a gang. The principal threatened expulsion. It hadn't gotten better; it had gotten worse.

Hope again: Desperate for help, we put him in a Christian residential program. He was safe from his bad choices. He came to Christ. He learned Scripture. He got counseling. He came out determined to walk with God.

Despair again: He got back with his old friends. A driver's license gave him too much freedom; he skipped school and was caught up in drugs, alcohol, and girls.

It was an ongoing cycle of hope and despair. I know you have been there.

Our natural response: *I give up. There is no hope. Nothing makes a difference. I can't do this anymore.* Others say, "Hang in there. Don't give up."

Hanging on is exhausting.

God tells us, *Persevere.*

"And let us run with perseverance the race marked out for us, fixing our eyes on Jesus, the pioneer and perfecter of faith. For the joy set before him he endured the cross, scorning its shame, and sat down at the right hand of the throne of God. Consider him who endured such opposition from sinners, so that you will not grow weary and lose heart" (Hebrews 12:1–3).

"So do not throw away your confidence; it will be richly rewarded. You need to persevere so that when you have done the will of God, you will receive what he has promised" (Hebrews 10:35–36).

There is rest in persevering. God knows we can't do it ourselves. So He stays with us and shows us how. He completely "hangs in there" with us—strengthening our grip, enabling us to endure, filling us with hope, covering us with grace, flooding us with peace. He perseveres *with us* so that *we* can persevere.

RESPONSE:

1. In your own experience, what is the difference between hanging on and persevering? What does each approach look like?

2. What truth do you need to keep fixed in your own mind to allow God to persevere with you?

DAY 36: Rest in Listening

I'm sure you have had the experience of your prodigal not listening to you. You have given every kind of love, encouragement, admonition, and consequence you can think of. He just doesn't listen.

So you decide to be quiet. Of course, you pray.

And sometimes your silence can be the turning point. Your prodigal seeks you out. Suddenly he has ears to hear, and he welcomes your voice in his life.

For others, and at other times, it doesn't change. She is stubborn. It grows worse. Perhaps you come to a point of intervention. For a child, you remove significant things in her life—a car, a phone, video games. Or you put her in a program. Or you tell her that her choices indicate she has decided to move out of your home. Perhaps with an adult you seek enrollment in rehab. Or you get a restraining order.

Sometimes it takes drastic action to get a prodigal's attention and produce change.

Sigh. Sometimes God does the same with us.

He speaks words of love, encouragement, and admonition, and provides consequences for us. But we don't listen.

So He grows silent.

Closing up our ears to the Lord is exhausting.

Be assured; He has not left us. Jesus and the Holy Spirit are praying for us. Hopefully, His silence will be a turning point for us. And we will realize we are missing His fellowship, peace, and wisdom. That we are missing whatever we need that comes when we are abiding in Him.

But of course some of us are stubborn. And God needs to stage an intervention, something more drastic to get our attention. Hopefully, we listen to what He is saying to us.

As we come back to Him, He says, "Be still, and know that I am God" (Psalm 46:10).

There is rest in listening.

RESPONSE:

1. When you first realized this section was about listening, did you think it would only be about your prodigal? How did you relate to the description of God's desire for us to listen to Him?

2. Recall a time when God had to intervene in order to get your attention.

DAY 37: Rest in the Promises

God is a promise keeper.

He has invited us to believe Him, to trust that He keeps His word (note which words are emphasized!):

- "Therefore, since the **promise** of entering his rest still stands, let us be careful that none of you be found to have fallen short of it" (Hebrews 4:1).

- "Does he speak and then not act? Does he **promise** and not fulfill? (Numbers 23:19).

- "Sustain me, my God, according to your **promise**, and I will live; do not let my hopes be dashed" (Psalm 119:116).

- "Peter replied, 'Repent and be baptized, every one of you, in the name of Jesus Christ for the forgiveness of your sins. And you will receive the gift of the Holy Spirit. The **promise** is for you and your children and for all who are far off—for all whom the Lord our God will call'" (Acts 2:38–39).

- "The Lord is not slow in keeping his **promise**, as some understand slowness. Instead he is patient with you, not wanting anyone to perish, but everyone to come to repentance" (2 Peter 3:9).

- "For no matter how many **promises** God has made, they are 'Yes' in Christ. And so through him the 'Amen' is spoken by us to the glory of God" (2 Corinthians 1:20).

- "Blessed is she who has believed that the Lord would fulfill his **promises** to her!" (Luke 1:45).

- "Know therefore that the LORD your God is God; he is the faithful God, keeping his **covenant** of love to a thousand generations of those who love him and keep his commandments" (Deuteronomy 7:9).

- "The LORD is trustworthy in all he **promises** and faithful in all he does" (Psalm 145:13).

I want to believe His promises, but sometimes it seems like He is *not* keeping His word.

Unfulfilled promises are exhausting.

A few things we *can* know: His answers rarely look like what we had in mind. His plan is always better. He is working on *us* even as He works on our *prodigals.* He is up to something bigger and better. And His timing is seldom our timing.

Through the years with our prodigal, as I read Scripture and sought the Lord, I claimed promises from God for our son. Did God say, "This is a promise for Josh"? Sometimes. But usually the Scriptures reflected work God had done in history or wanted to do in His children. Over many years, I have turned these promises from the past into prayers for our son.

Have they all come true? No, but some have. Are the answers what I imagined? No. But is there strong evidence of God's powerful work in Josh's life, along the lines I have prayed? Oh yes.

There is rest in the promises of God.

Here are some of the promises I have claimed and prayed for Josh. I have included the verse or paraphrase and reference, so you will know where to find each one. Maybe they will be promises for you to hold on to as well.

Prayer Promises for Josh

- Before you were born, I called you. You are my servant in whom I will display my splendor (Isaiah 49:1, 3).

- "Listen to me. . . . you whom I have upheld since your birth, and have carried since you were born. . . . I will sustain you and I will rescue you" (Isaiah 46:3–4).

- I am your redeemer. I will teach you what is best. If you obey me, your peace will be like a river and your well-being like the waves of the sea (Isaiah 48:17–18).

- "I have swept away your offenses like a cloud, your sins like the morning mist. Return to me, for I have redeemed you" (Isaiah 44:22).

- "Do not fear, for I have redeemed you; I have summoned you by name; you are mine" (Isaiah 43:1).

- "Forget the former things; do not dwell on the past. See, I am doing a new thing!" (Isaiah 43:18).

- "The people I formed for myself, that they may proclaim my praise" (Isaiah 43:21).

- I have called you. "I have chosen you and have not rejected you" (Isaiah 41:9).

- "I will strengthen you and help you" (Isaiah 41:10).

- "I will give you a new heart and put a new spirit in you. . . . I will put my Spirit in you and move you to follow my decrees" (Ezekiel 36:26–27).

- "I will put breath in you, and you will come to life. . . . Then you will know that I am the LORD" (Ezekiel 37:6).

- "Be strong and courageous." Do not be terrified or discouraged, for I will be with you wherever you go (Joshua 1:9).

- "I am the LORD; in its time I will do this swiftly" (Isaiah 60:22).

Our God has much experience loving prodigals—He loves us. He goes with us on this journey. He comforts us and gives us hope. He relieves our fears.

And He gives rest—for our weary bodies, our depleted energy, our tired minds, our exhausted emotions.

Let's accept His amazing offer, for in it is an amazing promise: "Come to me, all you who are weary and burdened, and I will give you rest" (Matthew 11:28).

RESPONSE:

1. When have you come to understand that God's answers rarely look like what you had in mind, but actually turned out better than yours would have?
2. Which promise quoted in this chapter touched your heart most profoundly? Why?

5

TRUST

You will keep in perfect peace those whose minds are steadfast, because they trust in you.

Isaiah 26:3

Trust is certainly an issue when you love a prodigal, isn't it? In addition to their lies and attempted deceptions, and our pain that they no longer trust and honor us, we ask the most important question: Can I truly trust God on this journey of living with and loving a prodigal?

In this chapter I hope we can deepen our trust in God in our daily walk, and especially as we love and interact with our prodigals. Brennan Manning, with his book *Ruthless Trust*,[1] has had a profound impact on my life and has been helpful on this topic.

Time and again Manning has sent me to God's Word, and that is what we will do here: go to the Word. We will consider not only *why* we can trust God, but *how* we can trust Him. And we will look at how that trust will affect our lives and our loved ones.

Manning defines trust as faith in action; trust is something we *do*. Let's explore what this action of trust is.

We will begin by intentionally focusing on the following words from God, words that will establish our hearts on Him and prepare us to be able to trust Him at all times. We have considered some of these before; this time, let us ponder them in the light of God's trustworthiness.

- "So do not fear, for I am with you; do not be dismayed, for I am your God. I will strengthen you and help you; I will uphold you with my righteous right hand" (Isaiah 41:10).
- "When I am afraid, I put my trust in you" (Psalm 56:3).
- "I remain confident of this: I will see the goodness of the Lord in the land of the living. Wait for the Lord; be strong and take heart and wait for the Lord" (Psalm 27:13–14).
- "The Lord himself goes before you and will be with you; he will never leave you nor forsake you. Do not be afraid; do not be discouraged" (Deuteronomy 31:8).

The more we know someone, the better we can judge if they are trustworthy. So let's get to know God—and I believe we will find that we can trust Him.

DAY 38: Trust and the Glory of God

The first reality of God that will help us trust Him is His glory.

I recently experienced a few weeks with the glory of God: The grandeur of the Colorado mountains. The peaceful beauty of bluebonnet-clad Texas hill country. The faces of my grandchildren.

Even my own reflection in the mirror. What? Yes, my own face, for we are a reflection of the glory of God.

All of these, and the amazing glory of creation all around us, are just shadowy hints at the glory of God.

The Hebrew word for the glory of God is *kabod*. It is a comprehensive word with many shades of meaning. The most basic definition is "weight." It can connote heaviness, wealth, rank, status, power. To the children of Israel it meant the greatness, eminence, power, authority, and majesty of God. Even those weighty words were insufficient to capture the glory of God. A greater description could be "a light so brilliant that Yahweh Himself is rendered invisible by the brilliance."[2] (See also Ezekiel 1:28; 3:12, 23; 8:4; 10:18ff.)

His Glory Revealed

Moses wanted to see the face of God—the glory of God—but God said no. Moses could see only God's back, "for no one may see me and live" (Exodus 33:20).

Yet we *can* see Him. Jesus reveals the Father—He is the Light of the world who shares in the luminous brilliance of His father. He tells us that, when we see Him, we see the Father (John 14:9).

When John was transported in his revelation vision, he recorded,

I turned around to see the voice that was speaking to me. And when I turned I saw seven golden lampstands, and among the lampstands was someone like a son of man, dressed in a robe reaching down to his feet and with a golden sash around his chest. The hair on his head was white like wool, as white as snow, and his eyes were like blazing fire. His feet were like bronze glowing in a furnace, and his voice was like the sound of rushing waters. In his right hand he held seven stars, and coming out of his mouth was a sharp, double-edged sword. His face was like the sun shining in all its brilliance. When I saw him, I fell at his feet as though dead.

Revelation 1:12–17

John did just what we should do when we get even a small glimpse of God, when we experience hints of His glory: He fell on his face, and so should we.

Growing in Seeing His Glory

Too often I settle for such a small comprehension of God and His glory. I think most of us accept a puny picture of our great God. Though we don't have the capacity to see the full glory of God, He does reveal himself to us in many ways. The magnificence of creation and the beauty of those made in His image—you and I—show His glory and loveliness most profoundly.

Every time we see God's faithfulness in being true to His own character, we catch a glimpse of that glory. Each time we discover that He is with us, that He loves and accepts us and keeps His promises, we once again grasp that He is trustworthy. Whenever we receive answers to prayer and surprise gifts from Him, we understand that He is faithful.

We recognize that we can trust Him.

As we walk on the wilderness path of loving a prodigal, our only hope of surviving and thriving is to know that we can trust God. Our only hope of wooing our loved ones back to God—and to us—is to let the light and glory of God shine through us.

RESPONSE:

1. When have you had an especially vivid glimpse of the glory of God?
2. How do you think growing in your view of God's glory will help you love and pray for your prodigal?

DAY 39: Trust and the "Godness" of God

If we are to trust God in this challenging journey with our prodigals, we need to see that He is trustworthy. Even in the face of pain and suffering—the kind of pain that raises questions and doubts within us—God is utterly and completely trustworthy. Let's discover, grasp, and know this trustworthy God more than ever.

So far in this chapter, we've gotten a tiny glimpse of God's glory. Let's go further and let Him speak for himself—to tell us a little of who He is. Along the way, I will attempt to bring these words home to us regarding our lives with prodigals.

Names God Gives Himself

All the names of God in the Bible give us pictures of what He is like. Different authors of the books of the Bible identify Him with different names. But sometimes God himself tells us His name. Here are a few of those:

I AM

"God said to Moses, 'I AM WHO I AM. This is what you are to say to the Israelites: "I AM has sent me to you"'" (Exodus 3:14). God is the eternal present tense. He has no beginning or ending. He is here with us. Always.

El Emunah—The Faithful God

"Know therefore that the LORD your God is God; he is the faithful God, keeping his covenant of love to a thousand generations of those who love him and keep his commands" (Deuteronomy 7:9). Scripture also tells us that God must be faithful because He must be true to who He is (2 Timothy 2:13).

El Gibor—The Mighty God

"For the LORD your God is God of gods and Lord of lords, the great God, mighty and awesome, who shows no partiality and accepts no bribes" (Deuteronomy 10:17).

In God's conversation with Moses, when He gives the Ten Commandments a second time, He reminds Moses that He is a mighty God. The children of Israel had just made and worshiped a golden calf—a paltry idol. But we don't love and serve an idol; we love and serve the true, mighty, and awesome God.

Jehovah Rapha—God the Healer

"He said, 'If you listen carefully to the LORD your God and do what is right in his eyes, if you pay attention to his commands and keep all his decrees, I will not bring on you any of the diseases I brought on the Egyptians, for I am the LORD, who heals you'" (Exodus 15:26). Certainly we and our prodigals are in need of healing—and God can do that.

Jehovah Tsidkenu—God Our Righteousness

"Say to the Israelites, 'You must observe my Sabbaths. This will be a sign between me and you for the generations to come, so you may know that I am the LORD, who makes you holy'" (Exodus 31:13). We know we can't make ourselves holy, and our loved ones are far from holy also. But God imparts His righteousness to us.

These names of God give us just a small picture of His magnificence and His gifts to us. There is much more about God's names in chapter 7, "Promise," but in the meantime, let's consider another image of God's "Godness."

God Speaks to Job

After Job has suffered greatly both from Satan's attacks and his friends' words, God himself comes to Job with a dizzying interrogation. Job chapters 38 through 40 are pure poetry, profoundly reminding us that our God is beyond our comprehension. Here are the first verses of Job 38:

> Then the Lord answered Job out of the storm. He said:
>
> "Who is this that darkens my counsel
>   with words without knowledge?
> Brace yourself like a man;
>   I will question you,
>   and you shall answer me.
>
> Where were you when I laid the earth's foundation?
>   Tell me, if you understand.
> Who marked off its dimensions? Surely you know!
>   Who stretched a measuring line across it?
> On what were its footings set,
>   or who laid its cornerstone—
> while the morning stars sang together
>   and all the angels shouted for joy?
>
> Who shut up the sea behind doors
>   when it burst forth from the womb,
> when I made the clouds its garment
>   and wrapped it in thick darkness,
> when I fixed limits for it
>   and set its doors and bars in place,
> when I said, 'This far you may come and no farther;
>   here is where your proud waves halt'?
>
> Have you ever given orders to the morning,
>   or shown the dawn its place,

that it might take the earth by the edges
    and shake the wicked out of it? . . .

What is the way to the abode of light?
    And where does darkness reside?
Can you take them to their places?
    Do you know the paths to their dwellings?
Surely you know, for you were already born!
    You have lived so many years!

Have you entered the storehouses of the snow
    or seen the storehouses of the hail,
which I reserve for times of trouble,
    for days of war and battle?
What is the way to the place where the lightning is
    dispersed,
    or the place where the east winds are scattered over
      the earth?
Who cuts a channel for the torrents of rain,
    and a path for the thunderstorm,
to water a land where no man lives,
    a desert with no one in it,
to satisfy a desolate wasteland
    and make it sprout with grass?
Does the rain have a father?
    Who fathers the drops of dew?
From whose womb comes the ice?
    Who gives birth to the frost from the heavens
when the waters become hard as stone,
    when the surface of the deep is frozen?"

Job 38:1–13, 19–30 NIV1984

Finally, in Job 40:1, God pauses and says to Job, "Will the one who contends with the Almighty correct him? Let him who accuses God answer him!"

Job's response: "I am unworthy—how can I reply to you? I put my hand over my mouth. I spoke once, but I have no answer—twice, but I will say no more" (Job 40:2–5 NIV1984).

I imagine that Job fell on his face, joining Moses, Joshua, Daniel, John, and others when confronted with the incomprehensible reality of God.

As should we.

RESPONSE:

1. Review the names God calls himself. Which one means the most to you today? Why?
2. The same God who gave Job a tutorial on His vastness and power is also the one who keeps a covenant of love with you. How might this truth help instill in you a deeper trust of God?

DAY 40: Trust and the Goodness of God

Certainly, as lovers of prodigals, we sense at least two hard things threatening our grasp on the goodness of God: Our constant exposure—in this age of instant information—to the horror going on in the world; and our frequent struggle with so much pain, fear, confusion. And doubt.

We ask: Is God really good?

We have loved ones we are praying for who go to prison, destroy their lives with drugs and alcohol, and even take their own lives. We seek help for those with mental illness and we raise the children our prodigals are unable to care for . . . and so much more. Where is God in all of this?

The first two parts of this chapter gave tiny glimpses of the blinding glory of God and the reality of His unfathomable "Godness." Hopefully our minds and hearts have been so expanded by the "so much more" that God is and does that we have made a place—a space—for believing that He is truly good.

Here are some helps for us in doing that.

God's Word Reveals His Goodness

Over and over, Scripture assures us that God is good and that all He does is good. Here are just a few of those promises:

- "I will make an everlasting covenant with them: I will never stop doing good to them, and I will inspire them to fear me, so that they will never turn away from me. I will rejoice in doing them good and will assuredly plant them in this land with all my heart and soul" (Jeremiah 32:40–41).

- "When all the Israelites saw the fire coming down and the glory of the LORD above the temple, they knelt on the pavement with their faces to the ground, and they worshiped and gave thanks to the LORD, saying, 'He is good: his love endures forever'" (2 Chronicles 7:3).

- "Taste and see that the LORD is good; blessed is the one who takes refuge in him" (Psalm 34:8).

- "You, LORD, are forgiving and good, abounding in love to all who call to you" (Psalm 86:5).

- "For the LORD is good and his love endures forever; his faithfulness continues through all generations" (Psalm 100:5).

- ". . . who satisfies your desires with good things so that your youth is renewed like the eagle's" (Psalm 103:5).

- "You are good, and what you do is good; teach me your decrees" (Psalm 119:68).

- "The LORD is good to all; he has compassion on all he has made" (Psalm 145:9).

God Works for Our Good in Ways We Cannot See

As my children were growing, I was truly intentional about doing good to and for them. They liked and appreciated many of the good things I did for them. Some they did not like—and said so. My good didn't match their good—but I was surely wiser than they were! Some of the good I did they never saw; I was always working for their good even when it was invisible. Hold on to that thought.

In a previous section I mentioned the book *Hinds' Feet on High Places*, the story of Much-Afraid and her extended time in a deep fog. She was assured by the Shepherd that He was still working, but in ways she couldn't see.[3]

The same is true for us. Our good God is always working for us and for our prodigals, even when we can't tell whether anything is happening or not.

God's Suffering Demonstrates His Supreme Goodness

Tim Keller, author of *The Reason for God*,[4] says the above thoughts are helpful but not enough. In his blog post "My Faith: The danger of asking God 'Why me?'" Keller reminds us that God's original creation did not include suffering and death. Those came by our choice to live for ourselves. Keller writes,

> But God did not abandon us. Only Christianity of all the world's major religions teaches that God came to Earth in Jesus Christ and became subject to suffering and death himself, dying on the cross to take the punishment our sins deserved, so that someday he can return to Earth to end all suffering without ending us.
>
> Do you see what this means? We don't know the reason God allows evil and suffering to continue, or why it is so random, but now at least we know what the reason isn't, what it can't be.
>
> It can't be that he doesn't love us. It can't be that he doesn't care. He is so committed to our ultimate happiness that he was willing to plunge into the greatest depths of suffering himself.[5]

Ultimately, God's willingness to suffer and sacrifice through the life and death of His Son demonstrates exceedingly a goodness in His being, His character, and His essence that is trustworthy!

Are we beginning to trust?

RESPONSE:

1. What do you imagine your good God is doing behind the scenes on behalf of your loved one and you?
2. How do Keller's statements about God's love for us and His willingness "to plunge into the greatest depths of suffering himself" help build your trust in our good God?

DAY 41: Trust and the Love of God

Many years ago I wrote a book called *He Loves Me.* The purpose was to explore whether or not I could consistently believe—trust—that God loved me.

The cover shows a daisy. The first chapter begins with a list of antiphonal good and bad circumstances, figuratively pulling daisy petals—"He loves me; He loves me not."

How many times have we who love a prodigal done just that?

We rejoice in God's love—"He loves me!"—when we see good progress with our loved one: not drinking in response to a disappointment, studying and making good grades, hanging out with better friends, getting a job and working hard, keeping his word. . . . But then we cry out our doubt—"He loves me not!"—as each new bad choice surfaces: She was caught shoplifting; he got his girlfriend pregnant; he drove high and got a DUI; she refused to eat and lost five more pounds. . . .

Our hearts and our minds can't comprehend how some of the choices and consequences we experience with our prodigals can be love. Does God love my child, my spouse, my sibling? Does God really love me? Can I trust Him?

Deep and Vast

Books are written and songs are sung about the love of God. As a new Christian in my teens, I was deeply moved by the song "O the deep, deep love of Jesus, vast unmeasured, boundless, free. . . ."[6]

Clearly, we can't do justice to that vast love, but let's at least take time to examine four realities that have the power to confirm to our hearts and minds (note the emphasized words) that God does indeed love us.

Proclamation of love: Has God actually said He loves us and our prodigals? Absolutely. Throughout Scripture, God proclaims His love for us, but nowhere more clearly than in John 3:16: "For God so **loved** the world that he gave his one and only Son, that whoever believes in him shall not perish but have eternal life."

Proof of love: It's easy to say it. But can He prove it? Clearly. Definitively. Incontestably. Unmistakably. You know the verse: "But God demonstrates his own **love** for us in this: While we were still sinners, Christ died for us" (Romans 5:8).

Promise of love: But love can be lost. What if my prodigal does something so terrible that I can no longer love her? What if he doesn't repent and return to God? Will God quit loving him? What if I do something so terrible that God quits loving *me*? Here's the promise: "For I am convinced that neither death nor life, neither angels nor demons, neither the present nor the future, nor any powers, neither height nor depth, nor anything else in all creation, will be able to separate us from the **love** of God that is in Christ Jesus our Lord (Romans 8:38–39).

Permanence of love: Seriously. God's love is forever. He says so in Jeremiah: "The Lord appeared to us in the past, saying: 'I have **loved** you with an everlasting **love**; I have drawn you with unfailing kindness'" (Jeremiah 31:3).

Can I believe that He loves me? Without a doubt. And my prodigal? Assuredly.

So can I trust Him? That's certainly where the question comes, isn't it? Does His love mean He is trustworthy, even though what He does or allows does not always seem loving?

Apparently, in His vastly superior knowledge and unfathomably truer love, He knows realities that are actually loving, even when they don't feel like love to *me*.

Personally, when the events and circumstances of my life become painful, confusing, crushing, I have to go back to what I know about God, to the truths we have looked at so far:

> I know that His glory is incomprehensibly greater than I can grasp.
>
> I know that He is God—mighty, sufficient, faithful, and the creator of the immeasurable universe.
>
> I know that He is good—in His very essence.
>
> And I know that our glorious, powerful, good God loves me.

Can I trust Him? Yes, I can.

RESPONSE:

1. Most of the Scriptures shared in this section are probably very familiar to you. Did any of them touch you in a fresh way? Explain.

2. Which of the four realities of God's love—its proclamation, proof, promise, or permanence—do you need today? Why?

DAY 42: Trust and the I Ams of Jesus

So we have now come to the real reason we can trust God throughout our wilderness journey with our loved ones: Jesus.

The Father loved His Son. In the last section we looked at Father God's love for us. And we know from the Gospels that the Father deeply loved His Son: "And a voice from heaven said, 'This is my Son, whom I love; with him I am well pleased'" (Matthew 3:17).

That assured love of the Father for the Son instilled complete trust within Jesus, who reminds us: "The Father loves the Son and has placed everything in his hands" (John 3:35).

Jesus trusted His Father. Jesus was so certain of His Father's love that Jesus trusted Him completely—to live and work and speak through Him: "Don't you believe that I am in the Father, and that the Father is in me? The words I say to you I do not speak on my own authority. Rather, it is the Father, living in me, who is doing his work" (John 14:10).

Even in the most terrible circumstances, Jesus trusted His Father: "Going a little farther, he fell with his face to the ground and prayed, 'My Father, if it is possible, may this cup be taken from me. Yet not as I will, but as you will'" (Matthew 26:39).

The I Ams of Jesus

Jesus modeled for us the possibility of trusting God as a result of our becoming convinced of His great love for us. But there is something more: He gave us all His statements that start with the words "I am . . ." We can find these "I am" declarations throughout the Gospels: Just as the Father is I AM and many other names describing who He is, so Jesus tells us He has many such names as well.

Each name addresses some aspect of human need. We all yearn for what will satisfy us—relationships, meaningful work, freedom from fear and pain, beauty, peace. Jesus offers us all that and more to meet our need

> **to be nurtured:** While we concern ourselves with the well-being of our prodigals, Jesus promises to watch over our own well-being. "**I am** the bread of life. Whoever comes to me will never go hungry, and whoever believes in me will never be thirsty" (John 6:35).

> **for guidance:** The path ahead is usually uncertain and can be extremely rocky, even dangerous, especially when you love a prodigal. Jesus tells us He will light the way: "**I am** the light of the world. Whoever follows me will never walk in darkness, but will have the light of life" (John 8:12).

> **for a Shepherd's care:** Sometimes we stumble. Others do us harm—physically, emotionally, in every possible way. Our prodigals leave the light, choosing the darkness. Jesus tells us He is watching, He knows our trouble, He will come after us—and our prodigals: "**I am** the good shepherd. The good shepherd lays down his life for the sheep" (John 10:11).

> **for strength:** Too frequently we forget where our strength and sustenance come from, and we try to navigate our life journey on our own. Jesus reminds us of the only way to make it through: "**I am** the vine; you are the branches. If you remain in me and I in you, you will bear much fruit; apart from me you can do nothing" (John 15:5).

> **for rest:** How weary we grow if we try it on our own! And how exhausting it is to keep loving a prodigal who is making destructive choices. As we saw in chapter 4, "Rest," Jesus is there for us once again, with this wonderful invitation: "Take my yoke upon you and learn from me, for **I am** gentle and humble in heart, and you will find rest for your souls" (Matthew 11:29).

> **for His presence:** In His presence, we discover what a friend, companion, and presence He will be for us every step of the

journey: "And surely **I am** with you always, to the very end of the age" (Matthew 28:20).

Once again, the question is: *Can* I trust Him? Oh yes, surely I can. *Will* I trust Him? With my prodigal, *for* my prodigal? With my own life?

Will I let Jesus be all that He says He is for me and mine?

RESPONSE:

1. Have you personally experienced a deepening of your trust in God as you have come to more fully appreciate His love for you?
2. Which "I Am" of Jesus speaks to a specific need you have today? Which one addresses a current need of your prodigal?

DAY 43: Trust and the Holy Spirit

We recently had another suicide in our praying community. It makes me angry. This kid wasn't on our list, and we didn't know we needed to be praying for her. Our enemy is truly a roaring lion seeking to devour our loved ones—and us. He comes to steal and kill and destroy. (See 1 Peter 5:8 and John 10:10.)

We know that God has promised to never leave us or forsake us. Jesus says He will be with us always. But sometimes the Lord seems so far away, and the pain is so very present.

I am grateful that God the Holy Spirit actually lives *in* us. *He* is the means by which we are never abandoned, never left alone, never forsaken. And He does many tangible things for us, including fulfilling the promises shared below. Promises like these carry us through our wilderness journeys, enabling us to trust God even in the darkness.

He convinces us of sin. A primary purpose of God's Holy Spirit is to convince us of our need for God:

> But very truly I tell you, it is for your good that I am going away. Unless I go away, the Advocate will not come to you; but if I go, I will send him to you. When he comes, he will prove the world to be in the wrong about sin and righteousness and judgment: about sin, because people do not believe in me; about righteousness, because I am going to the Father, where you can see me no longer; and about judgment, because the prince of this world now stands condemned.
>
> John 16:7–11

Needless to say, we are grateful that the Spirit is working in the lives of our loved ones, helping them to recognize their sin and their need for salvation and wooing them to the Father who loves them so.

He confirms our adoption. One of the Spirit's important roles is to assure us that we are children of God. He also works in the lives of those we pray for who have previously surrendered to Christ, but who have turned away from Him.

The Apostle Paul in the wonderful eighth chapter of Romans affirms this:

> For those who are led by the Spirit of God are the children of God. The Spirit you received does not make you slaves, so that you live in fear again; rather, the Spirit you received brought about your adoption to sonship. And by him we cry, "Abba, Father." The Spirit himself testifies with our spirit that we are God's children. Now if we are children, then we are heirs—heirs of God and co-heirs with Christ, if indeed we share in his sufferings in order that we may also share in his glory.
>
> Romans 8:14–17

He is our Counselor. Our first line of help for our prodigals is available anytime, anywhere. The Spirit of God is identified as our

Counselor: "I will pray the Father, and He will give you another Counselor, that He may be with you forever" (John 14:16 MEV).

So often we do not know how to help our wanderers, or ourselves. We need understanding and wisdom. Just think—we have available to us God himself to advise us, to help us to listen well, to guide our words and our actions. Often He will use human counselors in this process, but He also will speak directly to us at a time of great need.

For me, these wonderful gifts from the Spirit provide one more reason that I can trust God in the life of my loved one and in my own life.

The Holy Spirit also offers many other gifts and helps to us, which you will read about in chapter 9, "Spirit."

RESPONSE:

1. Which resource of the Spirit described do you need most today? What does your prodigal need?
2. How can you draw from the presence of the Holy Spirit to meet these needs right now?

DAY 44: Trust and Gratitude

There are times when I am a little whiny. So much travel, so many projects. I'm tired. All I can do is the next thing. It is hard to catch up, much less do the things that need to be done but aren't immediately essential. Little inconveniences are annoying.

See? Whiny.

Recently, when I was in a whiny state, I read a chapter on gratitude in Brennan Manning's *Ruthless Trust* and was sharply reminded of a lifestyle I have mostly chosen in recent years—gratefulness—but seemed to have forgotten in my weariness and whininess. Perhaps your prodigal has worn you out as well!

As we have been looking at all the substantial reasons why we can trust God, even in our difficult journeys with prodigals, we can benefit from some solid evidence that we are genuinely growing in that trust. Manning suggests, "The foremost quality of a trusting disciple is gratefulness. Gratitude arises from the lived perception, evaluation, and acceptance of all of life as grace—as an undeserved and unearned gift from the Father's hand."[7]

Consider the following characteristics of gratitude.

All means all. It is easy to make a list of all the blessings in our lives, for which we are grateful. It would be a good practice to do that daily.

But the kind of lived-out gratitude that is proof of our trust in God will also include saying, "Thank you, Lord," in *everything*—including those things we prefer were not happening in our lives.

Even for the pain caused by loving a prodigal.

Gratitude pays attention. The busyness of life, the bombardment of messages from our culture, and the challenges of the choices of one we love all distract us from an awareness of our God, who is active in every detail of our lives.

A heart of gratefulness stays aware of God in the beautiful events and joys, and in the difficult circumstances and experiences. This kind of gratitude pays attention to what He is doing, what He is saying, how He is working.

Gratitude is catching. You know those people you don't want to run into: the complaining, whiny ones with negative, ungrateful attitudes.

But you also know the ones who, in the midst of difficulties and disappointments, still exude joy and gratitude. You love to be with them, and perhaps you even "catch" some of that grateful spirit.

We tend to think that only joyful circumstances will make us thankful. In reality, joy—in *any* circumstance, good or bad—comes from an already grateful heart.

There is a God. Manning writes that gratitude focuses on God: "The theocentric character of gratitude is anchored in trust that there is Someone to thank."[8]

The word *theocentric* means having God as the central focus. We have certainly endeavored to do that in this chapter. We have affirmed that God is God; He is good; He loves us; and He has given us all we need in Jesus and the Holy Spirit. Hopefully, we have begun to see that God is totally trustworthy. He provides for us, meets our needs, stays with us, gives us strength, perseverance, wisdom—and hope.

As our trust expands, so will our gratitude. We will increasingly choose to "give thanks in all circumstances" (1 Thessalonians 5:18).

I love this thought from Brennan Manning: "To be grateful for an unanswered prayer, to give thanks in a state of interior desolation, to trust in the love of God in the face of the marvels, cruel circumstances, obscenities and commonplaces of life is to whisper a doxology in darkness."[9]

Can you whisper a doxology in the darkness?

RESPONSE:

1. What does your "doxology in darkness" look like today?
2. What part of a lifestyle of gratitude is still hard for you? Explain.

DAY 45: Trust and How to Express It

To this point we have reflected on *why* we can trust God. Now let's look at *how* we can trust Him. We will explore this by asking, "How do faith, hope, and love come together and produce trust?" Let's walk through this concept, step by step.

What do I have faith in? "Now faith is confidence in what we hope for and assurance about what we do not see" (Hebrews 11:1). Faith, in general, has been defined as the persuasion of the mind that a certain statement is true.

So here is the persuasion of my mind, my reality: I know I am saved through faith and I live by faith. When it comes to a hard place, like loving a prodigal, I believe God can do *anything*. He can save, restore, rescue. I do not doubt that.

But will He? Can I trust Him?

What can I dare hope for? God's Word encourages us to hope in what God has provided for us and assured us of: grace, mercy, forgiveness, eternal life with Him—and much more.

When it comes to my prodigal, though, my hope is more immediate: repentance, return, reconciliation. I hope that God will do what I want in the life of my loved one.

Faith and hope creating trust—our gift back to God. As we combine our faith and our hope, we learn to trust. Trust is our gift back to God.

Faith says: I believe that God is totally aware, completely compassionate, and all-powerful. I am confident that He knows, that He cares, and that He is able.

Hope says: I am hoping God will take all this pain, all these bad choices, all the worry and fear and hopelessness, and redeem it all, bringing His good out of this bad—these years of bad.

Trust says: No matter how bad things are, I can believe—I can trust—that God will intersect with this bad, engage in this pain, and accomplish what He knows is right and best. It may not be the outcome I hope for, but it is the outcome God desires.

God's love is the anchor. Remember what we have considered in this chapter:

God's glory is beyond our apprehension.

His "Godness" is beyond our perception.

His goodness is beyond our comprehension.

His love is beyond our appreciation.

That a God so glorious, divine, and good could love us so unfailingly, so unconditionally, so extravagantly is truly unfathomable. It is that unquenchable love that anchors our faith, our hope—our trust.

How we can trust God: Jesus became like us. He set aside His glory and Godness to live with us, totally entering into all of our pain and suffering. He demonstrated how to live dependent on the Father.

And so we would not be left alone and helpless when He departed, He sent His Holy Spirit to live in us—to comfort, encourage, teach, remind, pray for, give peace to, and empower us to trust! The Holy Spirit is life-giving, life-enabling, and therefore *trust-building.*

How we know we are trusting God: What do our lives reflect when we are trusting God?

We are grateful.

We are truly trusting God when we are increasingly able, no matter what the circumstances with our prodigals may be, to say, "Thank you, Lord." Then we see the evidence of our faith and hope merging into real trust. We find ourselves more readily obeying and leaning on Him rather than going our own way, trying to fix things in our own strength.

Who has demonstrated this kind of trust? Here are some examples:

Job: "Though he slay me, yet will I trust him" (Job 13:15 KJV).

Noah: "By faith Noah, when warned about things not yet seen, in holy fear built an ark to save his family" (Hebrews 11:7).

Abraham: "By faith Abraham, when called to go to a place he would later receive as his inheritance, obeyed and went, even though he did not know where he was going. . . . By faith Abraham, when God tested him, offered Isaac as a sacrifice" (Hebrews 11:8, 17).

Moses: "By faith Moses, when he had grown up, refused to be known as the son of Pharaoh's daughter. He chose to be mistreated along with the people of God rather than to enjoy the fleeting pleasures of sin" (Hebrews 11:24–25).

David: In spite of Saul's efforts to kill him, despite betrayal by friend and family, he said, "I trust in God's unfailing love forever and ever" (Psalm 52:8).

Daniel: Though threatened with death by lions, Daniel "went home to his upstairs room where the windows opened toward Jerusalem. Three times a day he got down on his knees and prayed, giving thanks to his God, just as he had done before" (Daniel 6:10).

Jesus: "My Father, if it is possible, may this cup be taken from me. Yet not as I will, but as you will" (Matthew 26:39). "Father, into your hands I commit my spirit" (Luke 23:46).

No matter what: Brennan Manning writes, "It requires heroic trust in the love of God to keep trusting no matter what happens to us."

He goes on to say that trust is the word that defines the Christian life, that childlike trust is the defining spirit of authentic discipleship.[10]

We want clarity, wisdom, assurances, promises. God gives those, but often they seem to be withheld because He has a higher purpose—that we trust Him. If we have those things we want, we are satisfied. We don't really need to trust.

But the heart of trust says, with Jesus, "Into your hands I commit my spirit."

How does our trust affect our prodigals? As our trust in God grows, and therefore our spirit of gratefulness expands, we will be different. Our attitudes, our countenances, our responses, and our words will reflect the grace and peace Jesus modeled. Our interactions and relationships with our prodigals will also experience more grace and peace.

Then this chapter's introductory Scripture becomes reality: "You will keep in perfect peace those whose minds are steadfast, because they trust in you" (Isaiah 26:3).

As we recognize that our fear and guilt often keep us from totally entrusting ourselves to God, we can understand that those we are praying for also have fears and guilt that keep them from entrusting themselves to *us*—as well as to God.

We deeply love those for whom we are praying. If we would multiply our feelings and our love by infinity, we would begin to get a greater glimpse of God's love for us—and for our prodigals. We would then become conduits for the amazing, accepting, forgiving, gracious love of God to flow through us to our wanderers.

We are God's arms of love to them.

RESPONSE:

1. How do you see evidence of faith and hope working together to build trust in God on your own journey?

2. When have you realized you had to practice "heroic trust" in regard to your prodigal?

6

PRAYER

Because he turned his ear to me, I will call on him as long as I live.

Psalm 116:2

When you love a prodigal, you will do just as that verse says—pray as long as you have breath.

You try everything: discipline, contracts, changing schools, counselors, professional help, residential programs, rehab—the list goes on. And some or all of your efforts might be helpful.

But when you can't escape the wilderness, you are desperate. You fall on your knees. You know He is the one who can help.

His timetable is rarely the same as yours. And you discover that He is just as desirous of working in *your* life as in your loved one's life.

You persevere. For me, in my journey with my prodigal, prayer became breath—an ongoing, intimate conversation with this God I was learning to know so much more deeply.

As you make your way through this prayer chapter, may you join with the children of Israel as they prepared to return from captivity, relentlessly petitioning our God, even as He told them:

I have posted watchmen on your walls, Jerusalem;
    they will never be silent day or night.
You who call on the LORD,
    give yourselves no rest,
and give him no rest till he establishes Jerusalem,
    and makes her the praise of the earth.

                                        Isaiah 62:6–7

DAY 46: Prayer Is a Mystery

I am a fan of prayer.

I believe in prayer.

I say often that "the work of God is done on our knees—then we find out what happened."

I facilitate a virtual global Prayer for Prodigals community.

Yet to me, prayer remains such a mystery. How in the world could the Most High God who created it all invite me to talk with Him, to make requests, to ask for His favor and His action on my behalf?!

How, indeed!

Yet He does.

He says: *Come. Ask. Confess. Inquire. Thank. Trust. Cry. Wait. Pray.*

He says: *All the time. Without ceasing. Without worry. Without fear. Without giving up. With thanksgiving. With faith.*

He says: *I will listen. I will hear. I will respond. I will answer. Wait. I have a better idea.*

He adds: *Ask for more—I have more to give. Ask for the impossible—nothing is too difficult for me. Ask for your heart's desire—I am already answering.*

He reminds: *Ask in my will. Check your motives. Be bold. Believe.*

Mystery, for sure.

I choose to walk with Him and talk with Him. To thank Him and bless Him. But I also cry out to Him and beg to know why. I believe and I doubt. I ask with bold courage and trembling fear.

God says: *You can move my hand. You can affect those you love and the world beyond. You can see miracles.*

He adds: *You have not because you ask not. Ask. I love it when you come to talk with me, to share your hurts and confusion and fears and hopes and needs and desires. When you open your heart to me. When you tell me how you really feel. When you love to be with me. When you obey and trust.*

We talk. I listen. And God listens and responds. He hears my prayers and He answers.

How can this be?!

Yet it is.

RESPONSE:

1. What is the mystery of prayer for you?
2. If prayer has become breath to you, what words do you speak the most frequently?

DAY 47: "Let's Talk about It"

"Let's talk about it." That was a favorite line from my five-year-old grandson. Mention anything—Star Wars, the playground, a snack, the latest book we had read—and he wanted to talk about it.

I find it amazing that any five-year-old would say, "Let's talk about it."

But that's what God says to us: *Let's talk about it.* After all, prayer is a conversation. He speaks and I listen. I speak and He listens. No texts or Instagrams or Snapchats. We just talk, heart to heart.

He and I have had many conversations.

When I am confused, He listens so patiently. Then He assures me that His wisdom, His mind, His thinking all are available to me. For some matters, it will be eternity before I see the whole picture, but His words give me what I need. He floods my heart with peace, for now.

When my prodigal has again broken my heart, God comforts me with His grace and hope. He reminds me that He loves that wanderer more than I do. He assures me He continues to pursue my loved one's heart.

When I am hurt, He shows me His hands, tells me about the pain of betrayal, then reminds me that His pain paid the price for all my pain.

When I have sinned, He tells me I am not condemned. I am forgiven. I am washed clean. Then He says to me, as to the woman caught in adultery, "Go and sin no more."

When I rejoice, He rejoices. When I laugh, He laughs. When I cry, He cries.

Sometimes He asks questions: *Do you know how much I love you? So how is your plan working for you? Will you trust me?*

Sometimes He whispers: *You can do this. I will be with you. I will never give up on you.*

Then He adds: *There's more, Judy. I have more for you.*

Always He is the answer, the end point of our conversation. He offers all of who He is to my every question, every need, every hope.

RESPONSE:

1. What specific things has Father God said to you in your prayer conversations?
2. What questions has He asked you? How have you responded?

DAY 48: The Lament of a Sigh

"Sigh."

How many times I have said, "Sigh"—with a deep sigh.

When my prodigal does the same thing again!

When an anticipated good outcome becomes not good at all.

When bad choices require hard choices of me.

When my prayers don't seem to accomplish anything.

A sigh often is a lament, expressing sorrow, yearning, weariness, resignation.

When our journey is ongoing and the wilderness is dense, and our prodigal keeps making the same poor choices, and the pain is weariness, we are deeply sad. We do sigh in resignation, despair, even hopelessness.

We make a lament, which is very biblical.

A lament is an elegy or a dirge. It verbalizes our mourning. And many times we are in mourning, lamenting the loss of peace and hope and dreams. Scripture has an entire book of laments: Lamentations.

God is not offended by our tears, our laments, or our sighs. He understands. He receives and treasures them. He reaches out to comfort and encourage.

He invites us to rest in Him. To transfer our burdens to Him. To trust His love and His goodness. To hope in Him.

It is then that a wonderful thing happens. My sigh changes. Instead of an expression of sorrow and resignation, it becomes my response to His invitations: a sigh of being understood and accepted, of leaning on Him, of snuggling into His arms, of resting in peace and even contentment.

Sometimes in my journey, just when I think my sighing is done, despair and fear return. The dirge resurfaces.

So I keep giving my lament to God and asking Him to transform my sighing from whispers of despair to exhales of trust.

RESPONSE:

1. When has your sigh become a lament?
2. When has it become surrender and rest?

DAY 49: Prayer Gifts

I look for any excuse to give gifts.

Sometimes just the right gift can accomplish just the right effect on a prodigal. But sometimes what she really needs can only come from God.

Once, as I was praying for our prodigal, God revealed to me seven prayer gifts that our son needed. These prayers may reflect just what your prodigal needs as well, or God may suggest different prayer gifts to you.

Prayer Gifts for My Loved One

Father, I ask you to give the following gifts to my loved one today:

Comfort: May he sense Your love and care and understanding even as he is in pain and despair over all he has lost, the betrayals he has experienced, the confusion about the future. Wrap loving arms of comfort around him (2 Corinthians 1:3–4).

Mercy: May he know that, because he is in Christ and seeking to follow Him, he has received mercy and forgiveness for *all* his sins—the past, present, and future. Assure him he is dressed in the righteousness of Christ and is welcome in Your presence (Isaiah 55:7; Hebrews 4:16).

Freedom: May he allow You to set him free. Loose the chains of all his anxieties, fears, curses, and addictions. May he be liberated from Satan's powerful strongholds in his life and live in freedom and victory (Luke 4:18).

Courage: May he see the foolishness of continuing to live in the misery he is experiencing—You have a plan for him that is so much better. May he have courage to choose to trust You, to turn from all that has kept him captive, and to believe that the path You have for him is good, even when it is hard, and that there is joy and purpose and meaning in Your way for him (Joshua 1:9).

Hope: May he turn from the despair and depression he is living in now and open his eyes and his ears to see and hear You— and perceive with great hope the good future that you have waiting for him. May this hope sustain him so he will not give up, but will press on in Your strength (Jeremiah 29:11).

Peace: May he be released from the things that keep him filled with anxiety and even panic, from regrets and disappointment, from the wrongs done to him, from abandonment and anger, from being a victim. May he instead be covered by and flooded with Your peace that surpasses understanding (John 14:27; 16:33).

Vision: May his heart and mind be opened to see what You created him to be. May he know he is not an accident or a mistake but rather a beloved child created by You because You desire him, want him as Your son, and love to be with him. May he understand that, while he was being formed within his birth mother, You were designing him for the good purposes and plans You have for him. May he be able to see glimpses of those plans and may he choose to walk toward them (1 Corinthians 2:9; Isaiah 64:4).

I not only prayed these prayer gifts to God, but I also sent them to our son so he would be aware of them and, hopefully, willingly receive them. (That may not be wise with every prodigal, but for us it seemed appropriate.)

RESPONSE:

1. What prayer gifts might you offer your loved one?
2. How could you be part of the answer to those prayers?

DAY 50: Battlefront Prayer

We all want to live in peace, don't we? But our world is filled with terror and war. Almost daily, enemies attack and kill. They can be frightening, unpredictable, deadly.

Yet we have a more powerful, more sinister enemy who hates us and has a terrible plan for our lives—and for our prodigals. Because he is unseen, we tend to forget about or ignore him. But we are warned in Scripture to be on the alert. We have seen that he is clever, looking for just the right moment, masquerading as good when, in fact, he is abominable.

While our natural tendency might be to cringe in fear or to run and hide, God's Word tells us to do just the opposite: "Submit yourselves, then, to God. Resist the devil, and he will flee from you" (James 4:7).

How do we resist the devil—for ourselves and on behalf of our loved ones? There are some simple but practical ways we can stand up to the demonic bully. The first two listed below help to prepare us to be strong to resist—in the moment and as a way of life—and to carry out the actions that follow.

Praise God. The evil one does not like hearing our God being lifted up, glorified, or praised. So we do just that, for Scripture tells us, "Yet You are holy, O You who are enthroned upon the praises of Israel" (Psalm 22:3 NASB).

God's glory and greatness are revealed as we praise Him. Praise Him in these simple ways daily or when you feel under attack:

- List His names, attributes, and qualities: He is good, faithful, loving, merciful. . . . He is God Almighty, Jehovah Jireh, our Shepherd. . . .
- Read aloud from psalms that especially praise our Lord, such as 95 through 100.
- Sing the Doxology.
- Sing praise songs.
- Read aloud from church liturgies.

Praise will send the demons scattering.

Thank God—in all things. Giving thanks in all things is probably the most life-changing practice I have learned. I have returned to this concept numerous times in this book because it is so vital to our trust in God and to our ability to resist the devil. When Satan has confronted or attacked, giving thanks has rescued me over and over again.

When I give thanks to God, especially in difficult or painful situations, several things happen: Almost immediately my perspective begins to change from negative to more positive. I am affirming to God that I trust Him to be who He is—God and good. I say it aloud so listening minions of the evil one hear that as well.

In addition, saying "Thank you, Lord" often is like handing God a key to open a door, and He will show me what He is doing.

Wear the armor of God. The Apostle Paul, in Ephesians 6, reminds us that the real battles in life are spiritual: "For our struggle is not against flesh and blood, but against the rulers, against the authorities, against the powers of this dark world and against the spiritual forces of evil in the heavenly realms. Therefore put on the full armor of God, so that when the day of evil comes, you may be able to stand your ground, and after you have done everything, to stand" (Ephesians 6:12–13).

Paul goes on to list the pieces of armor we are to be clothed in at all times: the belt of truth, the breastplate of righteousness, shoes of the gospel of peace, the shield of faith, the helmet of salvation, the sword of the Spirit—the Word of God—and finally, prayer in the Spirit.

Speak scriptural truth. When you sense you are under attack, when you feel oppressed and confusion reigns, speak aloud to the demons tormenting you, announcing the truth of Scripture. Choose to confront them with truth rather than making a power play.

Seek out verses that address the way you are being harassed. Quote scriptural promises, such as:

- "Being confident of this, that he who began a good work in you will carry it on to completion until the day of Christ Jesus" (Philippians 1:6).
- "The LORD himself goes before you and will be with you; he will never leave you nor forsake you. Do not be afraid; do not be discouraged" (Deuteronomy 31:8).
- "I am the LORD; in its time I will do this swiftly" (Isaiah 60:22).
- "Let us then approach God's throne of grace with confidence, so that we may receive mercy and find grace to help us in our time of need" (Hebrews 4:16).

Not infrequently I speak the following truths aloud: "Satan and all your demons, you have no authority in my life. I belong to God and am washed and cleansed by the blood of Jesus, adopted by the Father into God's family, filled and guarded by the Holy Spirit. You must cease, desist, leave—go where Jesus tells you to go." I speak the same on behalf of my prodigal, who has professed faith in Christ.

Walk in the Spirit. The ultimate means of resisting the devil is to make sure that I am consistently living in the power of the Holy Spirit.

Think about it: The Spirit of God comes to live in us as we put our faith in Jesus and His sacrifice for us. He offers us so many realities: comfort, counsel, encouragement, wisdom, reminders of what Jesus has said, help, truth, peace, presence, power. Whatever you need is available to you as you let the Spirit fill you, guide you, and empower you—every day and every moment, even as you are harassed by the evil one. (We cover this in greater depth in chapter 9, "Spirit.")

So when our enemy comes at our weakest moment, approaching us with subtle counterfeits of the promises of God, we can resist. God gives us praise, thanksgiving, the armor of God, scriptural truth, and the Holy Spirit so we can stand strong and resist the devil.

RESPONSE:

1. Which of these steps will help you resist the devil?
2. Where do you see the evil one attacking your prodigal?

DAY 51: Words of Blessing

When was the last time you spoke words of blessing into the life of your prodigal?

Blessings are the words of life.

Not long ago I read John Ortberg's book *Soul Keeping: Caring for the Most Important Part of You.* In it John shares abundantly from his years of being mentored by Dallas Willard. I especially liked the chapter on blessing: "The Soul Needs Blessing."

I've written a lot about blessings—and I've written a lot of blessings. I know blessings are a key to restoring the hearts of our loved ones to us and to God. But this chapter again reminded me of how important it is.

Ortberg quotes Willard: "Blessing is the projection of good into the life of another."[1]

Dallas Willard told Ortberg many times that the two ways we impact people are to bless them or curse them.[2] One or the other. Sometimes we probably are not aware of whether we are blessing or cursing, but we can certainly, intentionally choose to bless.

When I raise my voice, or give a sharp retort, or use "always" or "never," I am probably cursing. But I want to choose to bless—to encourage, affirm, speak truth with love. To speak words of life to my loved ones.

Here is a blessing for us from God—a very good place to start: "The LORD bless you and keep you; the LORD make his face shine on you and be gracious to you; the LORD turn his face toward you and give you peace" (Numbers 6:24–26).

Sometimes I have spoken these words and other blessings aloud, directly to my loved one. Sometimes he rejected the blessing in anger, but usually it diffused a situation or calmed him down.

More often my blessings have been prayers, or have been blessings of action, of grace and mercy extended.

I have written many blessings for people I love, often praying them for a person I care for. I usually ask God for the Scriptures I need to be praying for my prodigal or someone else. I turn those Scriptures into blessings.

Here is a blessing I wrote for my and all other loved prodigals several years ago. I pray it will give you the heart and words to bless your loved one:

A Blessing for a Loved Child

May you rise when you fall and come out of the darkness into God's light. (Micah 7:8–9)

May you be built up, not torn down; planted, not up-rooted. May you return to God with all your heart. (Jeremiah 24:6–7)

May you hope in the future of God's good plans for you. (Ephesians 2:10)

May you comprehend that it gives God joy to always do good to you. (Jeremiah 32:40)

May nothing of the world, the flesh, or the devil satisfy you, but only God. (Psalm 90:14)

May all the days and years of your life stolen by the evil one be restored. (Joel 2:25)

May the comfort, peace, and healing of God bring praise to your lips. (Isaiah 57:18–19)

May you feel cords of lovingkindness as the Father bends down to feed you. (Hosea 11:4)

May God pour out His Holy Spirit on you. (Joel 2:28)

May you know that in Christ Jesus there is no condemnation. (Romans 8:1)

May you be convinced that nothing can separate you from the love of God. (Romans 8:38–39)

May the eyes of your heart be enlightened that you might know Him. (Ephesians 1:18)

And may God bless you more than you can ask or imagine. (Ephesians 3:20)

RESPONSE:

1. How have you been blessed by the words or actions of another?

2. What blessings might you speak to or pray for your prodigal?

DAY 52: Prayers of Forgiveness

Our prodigal wronged us many times over the years: He lied to us, cursed us, stole from us, disrespected us. . . .

I am grateful those wrongs rarely impact our relationship now. How is that possible?

Because we have forgiven him.

Relationships require forgiveness. We are flawed people who hurt others—even those we love.

Scripture is abundantly clear that God wants us to learn to forgive, even though people have wronged us and don't deserve forgiveness. Paul sums it up with this instruction: "Bear with each other and forgive one another if any of you has a grievance against someone. Forgive as the Lord forgave you" (Colossians 3:13).

And of course, our model is Jesus himself, who said from the cross: "Father, forgive them, for they do not know what they are doing" (Luke 23:34).

We need to forgive the seemingly impossible-to-forgive things as well as hurts that happen every day.

What if they haven't apologized? Even then. But it's not easy.

In chapter 2, "Grace," I shared a prayer for forgiving, a prayer to help us take the step to release someone who has hurt us or offended us. Because of the magnitude of forgiveness, I am including it here again:

Father, thank you for your mercy and grace toward me, and for forgiving my sins through Jesus' death on the cross. Thank you that you forgive me over and over, for repeated sins and for new sins. I am so grateful for your grace.

Lord, I need to forgive _____, my loved one who has wronged me, hurt me, betrayed me, offended me, sinned against me. It is hard for me to do this—I am still hurt, angry, confused. So I come asking you for the power to forgive _____. Fill me with your Spirit and remind me of your love and mercy to me—and to _____.

By your Spirit, I choose to forgive _____. I choose to extend grace and mercy to him/her, even as you have done for me. I choose, as you enable me, to live at peace with this person I love. I ask that you bless _____ in your love. May we be reconciled and our relationship healed. And if that does not happen, may I continue to love and forgive.

Thank you that this is possible in the power of your Spirit. In Jesus' name, Amen.

We also need forgiveness when we have offended our loved one. Harsh words, degrading comments, unfair discipline, caustic attitudes can all damage the one we love as well as hurt our relationship.

Then *we* are the ones who need to ask forgiveness—from our prodigal. This requires the challenging choice to humble ourselves and admit offense, our sin. A simple conversation like this can help:

"(Your loved one's name), I was wrong to (name the offense). I know that was hurtful to you. Our relationship matters to me, and I desire to relate to you in a better way. Will you forgive me? Thank you so much."

There is one more person you might need to ask forgiveness of: yourself. Though we are often on the receiving end of wrong and offense, we still find ourselves saying, "I didn't handle that well," or even, "I really blew that."

So be sure to extend mercy to yourself as well.

RESPONSE:

1. Which is easier for you: to forgive or to ask forgiveness? Why?

2. Do you need to have a conversation with your loved one now—or soon?

DAY 53: Your Prayer Has Been Heard

David certainly understood our emotions in the battle. Over and over he asked, "How long, O LORD?"

"How long, LORD? Will you forget me forever? How long will you hide your face from me?" (Psalm 13:1).

I've said those same words. I'm sure you have too.

One of my hardest times came when it seemed my son was moving in a good direction—hope was being fulfilled, his life was changing—but then he reverted. Bad choices were made. Hope was dashed. Despair set in.

How long, O Lord?

Another person who surely must have asked that question, after seemingly unanswered prayer, while longing and waiting, is Zechariah. He and Elizabeth had pleaded for a child for decades. Then a word came from God: "Do not be afraid, Zechariah; your prayer has been heard" (Luke 1:13).

This message was delivered by a heavenly messenger assuring Zechariah that he had nothing to fear—and that his decades of prayer for a child had not fallen on deaf ears. *God had heard.* Now was the right time for God's answer. Zechariah and Elizabeth's son, John the Baptist, would prepare the way for the coming Christ.

God also has a message for us.

My emotions—in my "How long, O Lord?" times—lead to these kinds of thoughts and questions:

- Are you listening, Lord? Do you care?
- What about the promises? Can I believe you?
- I am afraid—afraid for the future of my loved one. Will change ever come?
- Is there sin in my life that blocks my prayers? Or am I just not effective at praying?
- Will hope ever be fulfilled, or will hope always be disappointed?

I could go on. I'm sure you have asked these or similar questions. But the right answer to these questions is not in things turning out the way I want, in my pain leaving, in my desired answer to prayer.

The answer is in God, in who He is, in what He is like. I can never understand all that He is doing or how He is working. But I *do* know He does all things well, He is good and is always looking for ways to do good to us, and His promises are true and can be trusted.

And I can know that my prayers have been heard.

In times that are often full of bad news and disappointment as we wait for an answer, may you know that God has heard your prayers and that His answers will be right and at the right time.

RESPONSE:

1. When have you doubted that God has heard your prayers?
2. What has helped you to believe that He has?

DAY 54: Your Prayers Live On

We have acknowledged the reality that we often grow weary of praying. We sometimes think the answers will never come, and we feel like we have no idea how to pray effectively.

Even after learning from other prodigal lovers, reading books on the subject, listening to sermons, and of course praying for many hours over the years, I still consider prayer a holy mystery. I just know I need to keep asking, seeking, and knocking. (See Luke 11:9.)

I have come to understand that my prayers do not end when I quit praying! Or even when I die! They continue into the future. I want to give you a picture to keep you on your knees: Your prayers are a sweet aroma to the Lord *until Christ returns.* Read these words from Revelation:

> Then I saw a Lamb, looking as if it had been slain, standing at the center of the throne, encircled by the four living creatures and the elders. . . . He went and took the scroll from the right hand of him who sat on the throne. And when he had taken it, the four living creatures and the twenty-four elders fell down before the Lamb. Each one had a harp and they were holding golden bowls full of incense, *which are the prayers of God's people.* (Revelation 5:6–8, emphasis added)

> Another angel, who had a golden censer, came and stood at the altar. He was given much incense to offer, with the *prayers of all God's people,* on the golden altar in front of the throne. The smoke of the incense, together with the *prayers of God's people,* went up before God from the angel's hand. (Revelation 8:3–4, emphasis added)

Your prayers and my prayers are incense offered to our Savior. The Lamb receives them as a fragrant, holy gift.

What you have prayed today for your loved prodigal will still be coming before God at that great day of revelation of the fullness of the glory of God. A day that we only dimly perceive now.

So all you have begged of God for your wanderer is still working! If you were to die before you see your loved one walking with God, your prayers have not died. They are still alive at the throne of grace.

Don't despair. Keep our King awash in the perfume of your worship, surrender, and trust in Him. Let the sweet aroma of your entreaties delight Him. May you be assured that He has received your requests.

RESPONSE:

1. How does it affect your heart to know your prayers will be a fragrant offering to Jesus?
2. Does this reality affect the way you pray?

DAY 55: We Have Prayed—Now What?

Everywhere I go I see ever greater evidence of the intensifying efforts of the evil one to capture hearts and minds—especially of young people—and carry out his agenda to steal, kill, and destroy. God calls His people to battle—on their knees.

And what a battle! I pray for my prodigal and for those loved by others. I am always exhausted when I finish an extended prayer time. We—and those we pray for—have an enemy who doesn't like that we are on our knees on their behalf.

God's Word reminds us: "But thanks be to God, who always leads us as captives in Christ's triumphal procession and uses us to spread the aroma of the knowledge of him everywhere" (2 Corinthians 2:14).

So after we've prayed long, speaking out everything we can think of to pray, what do we do?

We wait—to see what God is doing. Sometimes we will see immediate answers; other times we await the unfolding of change. God gives us glimpses of His response to our prayers. Some of us will rejoice in amazing transformation. Mostly we will wait.

We trust—that God heard and is answering our prayer. We have great assurance from God's Word that He desires for our prodigals to return to Him—and to us. So we take comfort from these verses: "This is the confidence we have in approaching God: that if we ask anything according to his will, he hears us. And if we know that he hears us—whatever we ask—we know that we have what we asked of him" (1 John 5:14–15).

We thank God—that He is moving even when we don't see it. We are admonished to give thanks in all things, even when we don't observe the answer we desire. We must remember that we look through that dark glass.[3] God is always working even if we can't discern what He is doing.

We give love and grace—as the hands and heart of our Savior to our loved prodigals. Our Father says He will woo them back with His lovingkindness.[4] We are His primary means of extending that love and grace that will, eventually, draw them back to God and to us.

We hope—because we have a strong anchor to hold our hope: Jesus himself. We remember that God's promises are all *yes* in Christ, so we have confidence to keep on hoping.

We walk in the Spirit—remembering and appropriating all that the Spirit offers to us: He advocates, encourages, comforts, reveals truth, liberates, gives peace, fights for us, empowers. We do this moment by moment.

And we pray—with hope, with perseverance, with assurance. We keep praying, asking God for release of His grace and power into the lives of those we love so deeply.

RESPONSE:

1. After an extended time of prayer, how do you feel? Exhausted? At peace? Expectant?
2. From the list of things we can do after a time of prayer (wait, trust, etc.), which is still hard to do? Explain.

7

PROMISE

The name of the LORD is a fortified tower; the righteous run to it and are safe.

Proverbs 18:10

Most of us have two, maybe three names, and perhaps a nickname. Each of us loves to hear our name because that usually means someone knows us, or cares about us, or wants us.

Sometimes we are named after a loved one, or our parents have chosen a name with symbolic meaning. Lately, names are often made up or put together from other names. However they originate, they become part of us. We are known by our names.

Our God is known by His many names. Every one of His names identifies a truth about Him. His names reveal who He is, what He is like, how He will act.

Each name is a promise.

Not a promise that He will do as we wish, but a promise that He will always be true to His name.

DAY 56: Call on His Name

When we need something from God, we can always come to Him "in His name." Our King, the God of the universe, has extended an open invitation for us to call on Him:

> God also said to Moses, "Say to the Israelites, 'The LORD, the God of your fathers—the God of Abraham, the God of Isaac and the God of Jacob—has sent me to you.'
>
> > "This is my **name** forever,
> > the **name** you shall call me
> > from generation to generation."
>
> Exodus 3:15, emphasis added

Throughout Scripture, God's chosen leaders knew to call on His name in their time of need:

Abram: "There he built an altar to the LORD and called on the name of the LORD" (Genesis 12:8).

Isaac: "Isaac built an altar there and called on the name of the LORD" (Genesis 26:25).

Elijah: "Then you call on the name of your god, and I will call on the name of the LORD" (1 Kings 18:24).

Our Savior, the Lord Jesus, gives us the same invitation: "Until now you have not asked for anything in my name. Ask and you will receive, and your joy will be complete" (John 16:24).

When God calls himself by a name, He is saying: "This is true of me."

When He calls himself Jehovah Jireh (Provider), He is saying that we can depend on Him to provide for our needs. Jesus was called

Immanuel (God with us), which assures us that He will always be with us.

Sometimes Scripture uses a specific name for God, such as *Shalom*, which is Peace (Judges 6:24). Other times He is described by a characteristic, for example, "God is love" (1 John 4:8).

The key is that we can trust God to be true to each name and each named character quality. As we move through our lives and are confronted by many different needs, we can call on God, by name, for that need.

RESPONSE:

1. How does this understanding enhance the practice of expressing your prayers "In Jesus' name"?
2. How is it helpful to you to use the specific names of God when you pray?

DAY 57: The Promise Is in His Name

The writer of Hebrews assures us, "Let us then approach the throne of grace with confidence, so that we may receive mercy and find grace to help us in our time of need" (Hebrews 4:16).

And the Holy Spirit goes with us as we accept the invitation: "In the same way, the Spirit helps us in our weakness. We do not know what we ought to pray for, but the Spirit himself intercedes for us through wordless groans" (Romans 8:26).

Jesus also prays for us. "Christ Jesus who died—more than that, who was raised to life—is at the right hand of God and is also interceding for us" (Romans 8:34).

So what are we waiting for? An invitation? We already have it.

God is on His throne, waiting for us to accept His invitation to come. His arms are open, ready to welcome us. His ear is attuned, eager to listen. His heart is open, desiring to respond. He will be true to every name He has called himself in the Word.

Let's look at some of the various names of God. Most will be from the Hebrew, with some from the Greek. Each name is His promise to us. Let us come into His presence, bringing our worship, our thanks, and our requests, with boldness and confidence, for He desires to be with us and to be all He is to us.

RESPONSE:

1. What is a name of God you need to call on now?
2. How does it reassure you that God has invited you to come to Him?

DAY 58: God Is Still in Control

My friend Debby Thompson tells of a joyful family sailing adventure that turned terrifying:

> Suddenly, without warning, three independent storms converged in uncharacteristic fashion and created the perfect storm. Black, eerie darkness descended, and we were the victims of a phenomenon at sea that no meteorologist could have predicted.
>
> In the blink of an eye, our lives were in grave and serious danger. Being 10 nautical miles out, there was no hope of shelter. Gale force winds, 60–75 miles an hour, threatened to crash us into one of the rocky islands. Howling wind swirled in a 360-degree motion; vicious waves soared 16 feet high; visibility was reduced to 50 feet. Lightning danced all around our craft, and our overwhelming feeling was one of utter helplessness.
>
> The look on (my husband) Larry's face confirmed our desperate plight. He was using all of his strength to steer the boat upright and to keep us alive. He cried out, "Oh Lord, save us, please save us!"

Have you been in such a situation, one that was totally out of your control? Perhaps a truly life-threatening encounter? Or the loss of a job—or worse, loss of a loved one?

If you love a prodigal, you know what it is to feel that things are out of control.

All of us love to be in control, especially of our own lives. The reality is, we are not in control. But thankfully, there is One who is. Two of the names God goes by are *El Shaddai* and *El Elyon*. They embody the truth that He is in control.

***El Shaddai*: God Almighty, the All-Sufficient One.** We first learn about *El Shaddai* in Genesis: "When Abram was ninety-nine years old, the LORD appeared to him and said, 'I am God Almighty; walk before me faithfully and be blameless. Then I will make my covenant between me and you and will greatly increase your numbers'" (Genesis 17:1–2).

Surely Abraham had no power to make this happen! But God was more than able to make him the father of multitudes.

We find this name of God used forty-eight times, most often in the ongoing conversation between Job and his friends. Job said, "But I desire to speak to the Almighty and to argue my case with God" (Job 13:3).

Of course, when he got the chance, he quickly discovered that God really *is* the Almighty! All-powerful and all-sufficient.

For those of us who—occasionally or often—feel powerless to do the impossible tasks God has given us, especially to walk through a prodigal wilderness, this strong name of God is foundational. Even in the most desperate days, we have the assurance that our God is in control and that He is able to do whatever is needed. Nothing is impossible for Him.

We can pray in the name of *El Shaddai* and see Him do more than we can ask or think or imagine in response to our requests. Nothing is too difficult for Him.

El Elyon: **the Most High God.** The meaning of *El Elyon* is "God is the high one."[1] Synonyms would be *sovereign* and *ruler*. In other words, He is in control.

This name of God appears throughout the Old Testament, but most often in the book of Daniel, in which we read the story of Nebuchadnezzar, the mighty ruler of the Babylonian empire.

Though he acknowledged the power of Daniel's God, Nebuchadnezzar still believed he, as king, was in control. Thus God's word to him: "You will be driven away from people and will live with the wild animals. . . . Seven times will pass by for you until you acknowledge that the Most High is sovereign over all kingdoms on earth" (Daniel 4:32).

And that is what happened. After seven years of living as an animal, Nebuchadnezzar looked to heaven and was restored. He said, "Now I, Nebuchadnezzar, praise and exalt and glorify the King of heaven, because everything he does is right and all his ways are just" (Daniel 4:37).

Is your life out of control?

Then it is time to acknowledge that. It's time to turn to this Most High God, to *El Shaddai* the Almighty, who is—in reality—in control. No surprises, no indifference, no "oops" for Him. He knows. He cares. He is able.

His name is a promise. You can depend on Him to be in control.

RESPONSE:

1. How is your prodigal making life out of control for you?
2. When has God demonstrated to you that He is actually in control in your life?

DAY 59: Our God Sees and Hears

Invisible.

God has given me many opportunities to interact with homeless people. Do you know the most consistent word they use to describe how they feel? *Invisible*.

Is that how you feel sometimes? Or even often? Invisible? I am so grateful that our God has names that assure us we are not invisible to *Him*. He sees and He hears. He sees what is happening with our prodigals and with us. He hears their cries and our prayers.

Please be encouraged with these reminders of His attention to our needs, and that God sees and hears.

El Roi: **He sees.** Sometimes we wonder where God is. Is He off taking care of wars in the Middle East, or earthquakes in Mexico or floods in South Asia? Is He attending to great political events? Or healing the multitudes of cancer? Does He even see *me*? Or this loved one for whom I pray?

That's how Hagar must have felt. A slave to barren Sarai and now pregnant with Abram's child, she is resented and abused by Sarai. So Hagar flees to the desert. There, an angel of the Lord greets her and tells her to return to Sarai, assuring her that she will have a son who will be the father of multitudes. Hagar responds, "You are the God who sees me. . . . I have now seen the One who sees me" (Genesis 16:13).

That same God, though He shoulders all the cares of the world, cares for us. He is *El Roi*, the God who sees. He sees our hearts for our prodigals, the pain they cause us, the despair that overwhelms us, and the fear that grips us.

And He sees our loved ones. He knows where they are, what they are doing, the pain they feel—and the future He has for them. Though they are out of our sight, they are never out of *His* sight!

Shama: **He hears.** We pray. And pray. And pray. Our willingness to pray assumes that someone is listening. But sometimes we wonder. Our prayers seem to hit the ceiling. We beg, beseech, cajole, bargain, and yet too often we feel like we have not been heard. We don't see the answers we desire.

But our God is a God who hears us!

We learn of *Shama* in the Psalms: "The righteous cry out, and the LORD hears them; he delivers them from all their troubles" (Psalm 34:17).

We can be assured that, as we cry out to God for our loved ones, He hears.

But there is more.

***Akouo*: He hears.** John tells us that our God is also called *Akouo*. He is listening and He is hearing: "This is the confidence we have in approaching God: that if we ask anything according to his will, he hears us. And if we know that he hears us—whatever we ask—we know that we have what we asked of him" (1 John 5:14–15).

This is present tense. Literally, it means that God *is hearing* us. He is always in the midst of hearing our prayers. What a promise!

Is it God's desire for these prodigals to come to Him? We know it is. So we can come to Him with confidence that He hears our petitions, our cries. He longs for fellowship with these dear ones more than we do. And He is, in His perfect way and time, lovingly drawing them to himself.

We are so blessed. Our God sees us and our loved ones—He sees it all. And He listens for our voices. We can be assured that His eyes are on us and His ears are listening.

RESPONSE:

1. When have you known that God sees and hears?
2. When you pray, how does the promise that God is paying full attention to you help you?

DAY 60: He Is Our Shepherd

Patches, one of my many dogs, was an Australian shepherd. She was beautiful and fun. And truly a shepherd. She was always trying to get us to go where she wanted to go. She would even approach a complete stranger, take his wrist in her mouth, and seek to lead him. This frightened a few people.

Jehovah Rohi: **Shepherd.** Sheep herders—shepherds—have responsibilities to protect, supervise, care for, and discipline their sheep. It is no wonder that God calls himself *Jehovah Rohi*: Shepherd.

We, His people, His sheep, need lots of protection, supervision, care, and discipline.

Take a minute to read through the most popular psalm of all time:

> The LORD is my shepherd [Jehovah Rohi], I lack nothing.
>   He makes me lie down in green pastures,
> he leads me beside quiet waters,
>   he refreshes my soul.
> He guides me along the right paths
>   for his name's sake.
> Even though I walk
>   through the darkest valley,
> I will fear no evil,
>   for you are with me;
> your rod and your staff,
>   they comfort me.
>
> You prepare a table before me
>   in the presence of my enemies.
> You anoint my head with oil;
>   my cup overflows.
> Surely your goodness and love will follow me
>   all the days of my life,
> and I will dwell in the house of the LORD forever.
>
> Psalm 23, brackets mine

What an incredible picture of what our God, our Shepherd, does for us. And then the Lord Jesus amplifies it: "I am the good shepherd. The good shepherd lays down his life for the sheep. . . . My sheep listen to my voice; I know them, and they follow me. I give them eternal life, and they shall never perish; no one will snatch them out of my hand" (John 10:11, 27–28).

I have held on to that promise so many times as I have prayed for my prodigal and for yours: "No one will snatch them out of my hand."

RESPONSE:

1. What part of the Shepherd Psalm speaks personally to you today?
2. What does hearing the Shepherd's voice and following Him look like in your life right now?

DAY 61: He Is Our Peace

Confusion. Turmoil. Conflict.

Every one of us experiences these in our day-to-day lives. And when you love a prodigal, they often become a way of life.

But I'm a fan of peace. I don't care for noise and chaos and especially conflict. I am a confirmed conflict avoider. So I am incredibly grateful that God has named himself Peace.

Jehovah Shalom: **Peace.** Gideon was no stranger to chaos and conflict. The Midianites totally oppressed and impoverished the Israelites. God's people lived in constant fear. Then an angel of the Lord appeared to Gideon, a youth in an insignificant family, called him a mighty warrior, and told him he was to rescue Israel.

Gideon apparently responded, "Pardon me, my Lord, but how can I save Israel?" After much conversation, the Lord gave him a sign, but Gideon was still afraid.

God said to Gideon, "Peace! Do not be afraid" (Judges 6:23).

"So Gideon built an altar to the LORD there and called it The LORD is Peace [*Jehovah Shalom*]" (Judges 6:24).

Our Savior confirms this wonderful promise to us: "Peace I leave with you; my peace I give you. I do not give to you as the world gives. Do not let your hearts be troubled and do not be afraid" (John 14:27). The Greek word for peace—*eiríni*—is comparable to the Hebrew *shalom*.

And Paul uses the same Greek word for peace in this amazing statement: "For he himself is our peace, who has made the two groups [Jews and Gentiles] one and has destroyed the barrier, the dividing wall of hostility. . . . He came and preached peace to you who were far away and peace to those who were near" (Ephesians 2:14, 17).

He is the source of peace, both for our troubled hearts and troubled relationships. So when our lives in the wilderness seem filled with chaos and conflict, we can call on the name of *Jehovah Shalom* and rest in the promise that Jesus gives us His peace.

RESPONSE:

1. What aspect of your current life needs more of God's peace?
2. How have you been learning that the peace God gives is "not as the world gives"?

DAY 62: He Is Our Helper

Surely when a mine collapsed on thirty-three Chilean miners several years ago, their first thought was terror—they cried out for deliverance. Their greatest desire was for help.

But help was slow in coming. For seventeen days many assumed the miners were dead. When it was discovered they were still alive, it was almost two months before it was possible to bring them safely to the surface—to escape the constant threat of death.

All of us have times in our lives when all we can say is "Help!" When we know God, our cry is more likely, "Help, Lord!"

God has a name that assures us He will help us.

Ezer: **Helper.** "Help, Lord!" is the right thing to say. For our God has called himself *Ezer*, God our Helper: "God is our refuge and strength, an ever-present help in trouble" (Psalm 46:1).

Moses named one of his sons in honor of God his Helper: "The other was named Eliezer, for he said, 'My father's God was my helper'" (Exodus 18:4).

The prophet Samuel named a stone marker to honor this same Helper: "Then Samuel took a stone and set it up between Mizpah and Shen. He named it Ebenezer, saying, 'Thus far the LORD has helped us'" (1 Samuel 7:12).

King Asa called on the same name of God when he heard that a vast army of the nearby Cushites had been seen approaching his kingdom to attack. "Then Asa called to the LORD his God and said, 'LORD, there is no one like you to help the powerless against the mighty. Help us, LORD our God, for we rely on you, and in your name we have come against this vast army. LORD, you are our God; do not let mere mortals prevail against you'" (2 Chronicles 14:11).

Ezer is a powerful word, with military connotations. It implies that God is a strong Helper. He is with us. He enables us to be strong and will enable us to stand firmly in our battles. He rescues us from our own choices, the actions of others that threaten us, or just from the daily risks of life.

God also helps us in many other ways: He gives wisdom. He enables us to love with unconditional love. He helps us to persevere.

The name of *Ezer* is used often in Scripture to assure us that God's help is always available: "We wait in hope for the LORD; He is our help and our shield" (Psalm 33:20).

And the writer of Hebrews reiterates this truth about our God: "So we say with confidence, 'The LORD is my helper; I will not be afraid. What can mere mortals do to me?'" (Hebrews 13:6). The Greek word translated *helper* here is *boēthos*, which is very similar in meaning to the Hebrew *Ezer*.

How wonderful to have such a Helper as our God for every need!

God not only delivers us from our fears, but He will also, as we call on this name of God, deliver our loved ones from captivity, from temptation, from addictions, from generational bondages. He is able to set them free, and we can ask Him to do so.

David encourages us again: "You are my help and my deliverer; you are my God, do not delay" (Psalm 40:17).

We don't understand God's timing or purposes, but we can trust that He is faithful to who He is, to the names He has called himself. He is our Helper.

RESPONSE:

1. In what specific ways do you and your prodigal need our Helper today?
2. How does He help you face your fears?

DAY 63: He Is Our Provider

Have you cried out to God for your loved one recently? Of course you have. What have you begged for? Rescue? Safety? Restoration? Hope?

Jehovah Jireh: **God provides**. God is the one who can provide for our every need and our prodigals' every need. He is our provider.

Consider Abraham.

The faith of Abraham was amazing. He followed a God he barely knew to an unknown destination. He believed that this God would provide the promised son as the first of a great nation; and God gave him Isaac.

But then, in Genesis 22, we see that God asked the impossible: "Then God said, 'Take your son, your only son, whom you love— Isaac—and go to the region of Moriah. Sacrifice him there as a burnt offering on a mountain I will show you'" (v. 2).

There is no record of objections or even questions from Abraham— just obedience: "Early the next morning Abraham got up and loaded his donkey. He took with him two of his servants and his son Isaac" (v. 3).

As they arrived at the place of sacrifice, Isaac asked, "'Where is the lamb for the burnt offering?' Abraham answered, 'God himself will provide the lamb for the burnt offering, my son'" (vv. 7–8).

We know the story. Abraham tied his son to the altar and raised the knife. But the angel of the Lord stopped him from killing Isaac. Nearby was a ram caught in the thicket. Abraham sacrificed the ram, and he named that place *Jehovah Jireh*—The Lord Will Provide.

Centuries later, the writer of Hebrews describes this event and adds that Abraham *reasoned that God could raise the dead* (Hebrews 11:19), believing that Jehovah Jireh would provide a resurrection of Isaac, the promised son, if necessary! No matter what, God would provide.

We can be assured that God is the supplier of our every need— even when He sees our needs differently than we do.

RESPONSE:

1. When has God given your prodigal provision, as a result of your prayers, without him or her even realizing it?

2. What is the most recent thing the Provider has given you?

DAY 64: He Is Our Banner of Victory

We can all agree that we are in a battle—a very real battle—fighting for the souls of lost people all over the world, including our own wandering prodigals.

In past sections we have talked about this battle, including the truth that love goes to war for our loved ones (chapter 1, "Love") because the enemy always looks for an opportune time to trip them up, while God offers them a "way of escape" (chapter 4, "Rest"); therefore, we must intentionally keep on our spiritual armor (chapter 6, "Prayer").

But we haven't discussed the final outcome of this war: victory.

Jehovah Nissi: **Banner of Victory.** When Moses and Joshua defeated the Amalekites, Moses used this name of God: "Moses built an altar and called it The LORD is my Banner" (Exodus 17:15).

It was the Lord who lifted high the banner of victory for them.

The idea of a banner comes from a military context. It was the flag that represented the authority to which a soldier owed his allegiance and under which he faithfully fought. It was the rallying point on the battlefield, and after a battle, a banner lifted high gave proof of victory.

God as our Banner reminds us that His ultimate victory over sin, death, and Satan was won at the cross (Colossians 2:15; Hebrews 2:14; Revelation 20:10). We have access to this victory now, according to these promises and many others:

- "The horse is made ready for the day of battle, but victory rests with the LORD" (Proverbs 21:31).
- "In that day the Root of Jesse [Christ] will stand as a banner for the peoples; the nations will rally to him, and his resting place will be glorious" (Isaiah 11:10).
- "But thanks be to God! He gives us the victory through our Lord Jesus Christ" (1 Corinthians 15:57).

- "No, in all these things we are more than conquerors through him who loved us" (Romans 8:37).
- "But thanks be to God, who always leads us as captives in Christ's triumphal procession and uses us to spread the aroma of the knowledge of him everywhere" (2 Corinthians 2:14).

So we pray and claim in faith the promises embodied in this name. He is our prodigals' victory and ours.

RESPONSE:

1. How might the image of God as your banner of victory shape your prayers today for your loved one?
2. When has God been your victory banner in your own growth as a believer?

DAY 65: Our God's Name Is God with Us

Alone. Overwhelmed. Stretched thin.

Sometimes these are the feelings we encounter as we continue on this journey with those we love. Others pray, encourage, share our burdens. But still we feel the weight. Amazingly, our God offers to carry it all with us, for us. He says, "You're not alone. I am with you."

In both the Old and New Testaments, we discover that God has revealed names for himself that promise that He will always be with us.

***Jehovah Shammah*: The Lord is there.** God, the Most High and Almighty God, makes the most remarkable choice: He dwells with His people—first in the Tabernacle and then in the Temple. In Ezekiel's vision of the New Jerusalem we see a new name for the city:

Jehovah Shammah. "And the name of the city from that time on will be: THE LORD IS THERE" (Ezekiel 48:35).

In the past and in the future, we can know we are not alone because God's very name assures us that He is with us, by His own choice.

Immanuel: **God with us.** In Isaiah, we see another name for God's presence with us: "Therefore the Lord himself will give you a sign: The virgin will conceive and give birth to a son, and will call him Immanuel" (Isaiah 7:14).

We are told by Matthew that this prophecy is fulfilled in Jesus: "All this took place to fulfill what the Lord had said through the prophet: 'The virgin will conceive and give birth to a son, and they will call him Immanuel' (which means, 'God with us')" (Matthew 1:22–23).

This is what the incarnation is all about: God became human so He could be with us in the flesh. Oh, but this presence of our God with us is so much more in Jesus. He is not just with us—He actually lives in us. He doesn't just dwell with us; He indwells us through His Spirit: "Don't you know that you yourselves are God's temple and that God's Spirit dwells in your midst?" (1 Corinthians 3:16).

Even as God dwelled with the children of Israel in a temple, now we actually have *become* the temple of the indwelling God.

So, though our wilderness journey with our prodigals may take us through dark nights, on rough paths, into scary situations, and beyond our own capacity to endure, God is with us every step of the way. He hears our cries, comforts our hearts, strengthens our resolve, and fills us to overflowing with His love and grace.

We have this promise: "God has said, 'Never will I leave you; never will I forsake you'" (Hebrews 13:5).

RESPONSE:

1. How is God's presence increasingly real to you?
2. How does knowing He is with you, and in you, encourage you?

DAY 66: God Is a Faithful Promise-Keeper

We have just looked at several names of God and the promises they embody. But perhaps we find ourselves asking, "Really? Do the promises come true? I haven't seen it happening."

Can we believe that God's names are promises? That He will be faithful to who He is, as defined by His names? Undeniably so. His Word says so. I shared this passage with you in chapter 4, "Rest," where we were encouraged to rest in God's promises: "Your kingdom is an everlasting kingdom, and your dominion endures through all generations. The LORD is trustworthy in all he promises and faithful in all he does" (Psalm 145:13).

Chapter 4 provided several Scriptures with evidence of God's faithfulness, even when confronted with the unfaithfulness of the children of Israel, of His followers through history, and even of you and me. I know I am grateful that God extends mercy and grace when I deserve judgment. Still He is there, always trustworthy, always faithful.

Here are more assurances of God's unfailing faithfulness:

- "I have always been mindful of your unfailing love and have lived in reliance on your faithfulness" (Psalm 26:3).
- "For great is your love, reaching to the heavens; your faithfulness reaches to the skies" (Psalm 57:10).
- "But you, Lord, are a compassionate and gracious God, slow to anger, abounding in love and faithfulness" (Psalm 86:15).

It is that same faithfulness that makes another characteristic of God unavoidable: He keeps His promises. His Word is filled with hundreds of promises—and He is good for every one of them, even the ones that don't yet seem fulfilled to us.

Rejoice in these good words:

- "God is not human, that he should lie, not a human being, that he should change his mind. Does he speak and then not act? Does he promise and not fulfill?" (Numbers 23:19).
- "Not one of all the LORD's good promises to Israel failed; every one was fulfilled" (Joshua 21:45).
- "As the rain and the snow come down from heaven, and do not return to it without watering the earth and making it bud and flourish . . . so is my word that goes out from my mouth: It will not return to me empty, but will accomplish what I desire and achieve the purpose for which I sent it" (Isaiah 55:10–11).

And oh, what promises our God has made to us: forgiveness, a relationship with God, abundant life and eternal life, peace, comfort, hope. . . .

And one more thought that I love—He hears and answers prayer: "The righteous cry out, and the LORD hears them; he delivers them from all their troubles" (Psalm 34:17).

A favorite story of mine is about Daniel, who had called on the Lord with many questions. When the answer finally arrives, delivered by an angel, I love the angel's assurance: "As soon as you began to pray, a word went out, which I have come to tell you, for you are highly esteemed. . . . Do not be afraid, Daniel. Since the first day that you set your mind to gain understanding and to humble yourself before your God, your words were heard, and I have come in response to them" (Daniel 9:23; 10:12).

We can trust our God to keep His promises. Paul tells us why: "If we are faithless, He remains faithful, for He cannot deny Himself" (2 Timothy 2:13 NASB).

May you know that God has heard your prayers and that His answers will be right and at the right time. He is a faithful promise-keeper.

RESPONSE:

1. What name of God has been most meaningful to you?
2. When have you seen God keep the promises in His names?

8

HOPE

May the God of hope fill you with all joy and peace as you trust in him,
so that you may overflow with hope by the power of the Holy Spirit.

Romans 15:13

When you love a prodigal, you know about hope.

It beckons. It's fragile. It's elusive. It's cautious. But rarely does it give up.

We so desire for our prodigals to be free from their bondage—from addictions, from rebellion, from sin, from mental and emotional torment, from wrong friends and wrong choices. We pray. We know that God loves us and our loved ones. Waiting with hope is what we have. But if we can't trust that hope, what do we have?

You know the answer. We have the Lord. We have a faithful Father, a compassionate Savior, and a powerful Holy Spirit. And the assurance that all the promises of God are "Yes!" in Jesus.

Can we have hope still? . . . Yet? . . . Again? Assuredly so! Will all our desires and dreams come to pass? Assuredly no. Will our prodigals break our hearts again? Likely so. Will we make mistakes as we seek to restore and reconcile? Without a doubt.

The only certainty we have is in God.

He knows: He knows your plans and your prayers for the days and years ahead. He knows your loved one and his choices. He also knows His own grand plan and how all this works together.

He cares: He looks at our prodigals and at us with tender tears. He feels the rejection, the loss, the disappointment. He stays with us through it all.

He is able: He is not a God who wishes He could help. He can help. He is *El Shaddai*, the Almighty. He rules heaven and earth. He said that *nothing* is impossible for Him.

So my challenge to you, and to myself, is to make God himself the object of our hopes and dreams. To seek Him above all. To entrust our prodigals and ourselves into His loving and able care. To surrender our plans, to believe His very good intentions, to trust His Spirit to give us everything we need with our loved ones.

Be encouraged by this promise: "God did this so that, by two un-changeable things in which it is impossible for God to lie, we who have fled to take hold of the hope set before us may be greatly encouraged. We have this hope as an anchor for the soul, firm and secure. It enters the inner sanctuary behind the curtain, where our forerunner, Jesus, has entered on our behalf" (Hebrews 6:18–20).

DAY 67: Hope in the Waiting

No one really likes to wait. In today's instant-gratification culture, waiting is especially challenging. And waiting with hope seems impossible to us.

King David had many opportunities to wait, and his experiences have helped me persevere through my times of waiting. Psalm 27 is such a story. I encourage you to read it. Let me lay it out for you.

The situation: David is in trouble. He is threatened by wicked assailants, enemies, war.

David's response: *I will seek the face of the Lord.* (See Psalm 27:8).

His conclusion: *I can wait with hope.* "I remain confident of this: I will see the goodness of the LORD in the land of the living. Wait for the LORD; be strong and take heart and wait for the LORD" (Psalm 27:13–14).

Defining some of the words and phrases in this passage will help illuminate David's message:

- "Remain confident": *aman*—believe, build up or support, render firm
- "Wait": *qavah*—to expect, to look for patiently, to wait for or on or upon
- "Be strong": *hazaq*—fasten on, seize, bind, conquer, be courageous
- "Take heart": *amas*—be alert, be courageous, fortify, establish, strengthen[1]

What I think David is saying: *There is trouble all around me. Enemies desire to destroy me. But I seek the Lord. And He meets me and rescues me.*

Therefore I am confident that my belief/trust in God is firm. I am connected to Him. I can believe that I will see God's goodness in the land of the living as well as in heaven.

So I can wait with hope. I can in my heart bind together the difficult present with a hopeful future (in this world) of God's involvement and goodness. I can live in the light of God—because of who He is and what He is like.

I will therefore be strong. I will seize and fasten on God and who He is. I will take heart and will bring my emotions, intellect, and will under His loving sovereignty.

I will eagerly anticipate what God will do. I will wait with hope.

Therefore I can say, and you can pray:

> *Lord, You know the pain I am experiencing because of the choices I or my child have made, or the pain life has brought. You know I want to trust and have hope, but I often am filled with hurt and fear and anger and even despair and hopelessness. But I will seek You, and You will meet me and rescue me.*
>
> *I am confident in you. I will stay connected to You and will choose to believe that I will see Your goodness in my life or the life of my loved one.*
>
> *So I can/will/choose to be waiting with hope. I will in my heart bind together this difficult present with that hopeful future of Your involvement and goodness. I choose to live in light of who You are.*
>
> *I will therefore be strong and take courage. I know what You are like—You are God and You are good. I choose to seize that truth and believe You will bring my emotions into confident trust and rest in You.*
>
> *I will eagerly anticipate what You will do. I am waiting with hope.*
>
> *Amen.*

RESPONSE:

1. When is it most difficult for you to wait with hope?
2. How does David's psalm help you to keep hoping?

DAY 68: Fear and Hope

When you love a prodigal, you live with fear.

My friend Dena, in her book *You Are Not Alone: Hope for Hurting Parents of Troubled Kids*, relates the time when she knew she had to confront her worst fears for her prodigal. She wrote them down so she could see them, acknowledge them, and face them. Here are some of the desperate fears she recorded:

I am afraid because Reneé could . . .
- be kidnapped and held against her will
- be abducted and sold into sex trafficking . . .
- disappear and never be seen or heard from again . . .
- move away, start a new life, and sever ties with us forever . . .
- suffer irreversible brain damage from her substance abuse
- die from alcohol poisoning
- die from an overdose . . .
- give up and commit suicide to end her suffering.[2]

Some of us haven't come to such extreme fears, but I know you have your own list of the worries that grip your heart, destroy your trust, and steal your hope. How can we hold on to hope?

Remember this verse shared at the opening of this chapter: "May the God of hope fill you with all joy and peace as you trust in him, so that you may overflow with hope by the power of the Holy Spirit" (Romans 15:13).

Yet fear sometimes overshadows our hope. What do we do with that fear?

We name our fears. We write down or say aloud what we are afraid of. That helps to take away some of the power of fear.

As we name them, we allow ourselves to weep, to mourn, and to lament the possible reality of those things we fear.

I find it helpful, after naming those fears, to offer them to the Lord, or lay them on the altar before Him. I usually just lift my hands up, figuratively holding up my fears, to give them to the Lord. I have a few times written them on paper and then burned the paper, as an offering to the Lord.

Another key for me to get free from fear is to say, "Thank you, Lord." For the things I am afraid might happen to my loved prodigal? Yes, even for those. Thanking God is so freeing. It opens the door for God to work in me and in my prodigal.

Then we can remember that Scripture contains 365 admonitions of "Fear not" or "Do not be afraid." One for every day of the year.

Let's look at a few of those Scriptures, spoken to some of God's servants who might have felt they had plenty of reason to be afraid:

> **Abram (Abraham):** "After this, the word of the Lord came to Abram in a vision: '**Do not be afraid**, Abram. I am your shield, your very great reward'" (Genesis 15:1).
>
> **Moses:** "The Lord said to Moses, '**Do not be afraid** of him, for I have delivered him into your hands, along with his whole army and his land'" (Numbers 21:34).
>
> **Joshua:** "Have I not commanded you? Be strong and courageous. **Do not be afraid**; do not be discouraged, for the Lord your God will be with you wherever you go" (Joshua 1:9).
>
> **Elijah,** when he had to tell King Ahaziah that he (the king) would die: "The angel of the Lord said to Elijah, 'Go down with him; **do not be afraid** of him.' So Elijah got up and went down with him [a captain] to the king" (2 Kings 1:15).
>
> **The disciples:** "But Jesus immediately said to them: 'Take courage! It is I. **Don't be afraid**'" (Matthew 14:27).
>
> **The disciples:** "Peace I leave with you; my peace I give you. I do not give to you as the world gives. Do not let your hearts be troubled and **do not be afraid**" (John 14:27).

Are our fears imaginary? No. They could come true in the life of a prodigal we love.

Will those fears return? Probably. New circumstances can trigger them. Our enemy the devil will send arrows containing those fears. We can again grow weak and weary.

Is hope real? Can it last? Will our hopes be fulfilled?

Hope placed not in our circumstances, nor in the restoration of our prodigals, but in God himself, is real. It will last. That hope will be fulfilled.

The prophet Micah tells of his hope, even in the midst of betrayal: "For a son dishonors his father, a daughter rises up against her mother, a daughter-in-law against her mother-in-law—a man's enemies are the members of his own household. But as for me, I watch in hope for the LORD, I wait for God my Savior; my God will hear me" (Micah 7:6–7).

RESPONSE:

1. Make a list of your fears in your wilderness journey.
2. Have you offered them to the Lord, who tells you not to be afraid?

DAY 69: Hope in Hard Places

When you love a prodigal, you will find yourself in some hard places. I remember times in the principal's office, in court, at juvenile detention, at the jail, in the emergency room, with a wrecked car. I know you can make your own list.

We have a kindred spirit in the prophet Jeremiah.

Jeremiah had a challenging job. He was repeatedly assigned to tell the children of Israel about the next dire events coming their way because of their constant sin and idolatry. His prophecies about bondage to Egypt, starvation under siege, and captivity in Babylon all came true.

He paid the price for the bad news he delivered. He ended up in some hard places: imprisoned, put in stocks, lowered into a well, attempts made on his life. No wonder he was called the Weeping Prophet.

But Jeremiah wept for his people. He also rejoiced when God asked him to pass on good news. See what God said through Jeremiah to those exiled in Babylon:

> My eyes will watch over them for their good, and I will bring them back to this land. I will build them up and not tear them down; I will plant them and not uproot them. I will give them a heart to know me, that I am the LORD. They will be my people, and I will be their God, for they will return to me with all their heart.
>
> Jeremiah 24:6–7

> "I will come to you and fulfill my good promise to bring you back to this place. For I know the plans I have for you," declares the LORD, "plans to prosper you and not to harm you, plans to give you hope and a future. Then you will call on me and come and pray to me, and I will listen to you. You will seek me and find me when you seek me with all your heart. I will be found by you," declares the LORD, "and will bring you back from captivity."
>
> Jeremiah 29:10–14

> "In that day," declares the LORD Almighty,
>   "I will break the yoke off their necks
> and will tear off their bonds;
>   no longer will foreigners enslave them.
> Instead, they will serve the LORD their God. . . .
>
> "So do not be afraid, Jacob my servant;
>   do not be dismayed, Israel," declares the LORD.
> "I will surely save you out of a distant place."
>
> Jeremiah 30:8–10

> "I have loved you with an everlasting love;
>   I have drawn you with unfailing kindness. . . .

I will lead them beside streams of water
on a level path where they will not stumble. . . .
Then young women will dance and be glad,
young men and old as well.
I will turn their mourning into gladness;
I will give them comfort and joy instead of sorrow.
I will satisfy the priests with abundance,
and my people will be filled with my bounty," declares
the LORD.

Jeremiah 31:3, 9, 13–14

"Restrain your voice from weeping
and your eyes from tears,
for your work will be rewarded,"
declares the LORD.
"They will return from the land of the enemy.
So there is hope for your descendants,"
declares the LORD.
"Your children will return to their own land. . . .
Is not Ephraim my dear son,
the child in whom I delight?
Though I often speak against him,
I still remember him.
Therefore my heart yearns for him;
I have great compassion for him,"
declares the LORD.

Jeremiah 31:16–17, 20

I will surely gather them from all the lands where I banish them in my furious anger and great wrath; I will bring them back to this place and let them live in safety. They will be my people, and I will be their God. I will give them singleness of heart and action, so that they will always fear me and that all will then go well for them and for their children after them. I will make an everlasting covenant with them: I will never stop doing good to them. . . . I will rejoice in doing them good and will assuredly plant them in this land with all my heart and soul.

Jeremiah 32:37–41

Nevertheless, I will bring health and healing to it; I will heal my people and will let them enjoy abundant peace and security. I will bring Judah and Israel back from captivity and will rebuild them as they were before. I will cleanse them from all the sin they have committed against me and will forgive all their sins of rebellion against me.

Jeremiah 33:6–8

Surely, as we who love a prodigal often find ourselves "in exile," in hard places, in fear, in rejection, hopeless—whatever that hard place might be—we can hear God saying these same words to us.

Yes, these words of hope were originally written to the children of Israel in their hard places. But the promises from God that Jeremiah delivers resonate through all of Scripture with the love, mercy, and grace of our Father to all of His children.

I love these evidences of God's love and care and intentionality toward me, toward us. I come back over and over to these words of great hope:

"I will never stop doing good to them. . . ."

RESPONSE:

1. What hard places have you experienced with your loved one?

2. What words of hope have helped you in hard places?

DAY 70: His Name Is Hope

When you love a prodigal, sometimes you lose hope.

In moments, days, and seasons of despair, we look for hope. Everyone, at some time, looks for a source of hope.

In an election season, people look with hope for a candidate to turn things around, or to restore order, or to lead with integrity. And many see no hope. In a financial crisis, how will we survive? Who will rescue us? Is there hope? When loss—of a loved one, health, a job, or a relationship—devastates, how will we go on? Can we keep hoping? Where do we look for hope? To family? Friends? A new job? A move? The government?

If we find no hope, what is there but despair, resignation, giving up? Hopelessness.

When you love a prodigal, you know these feelings.

When he comes home drunk once again. When she is pregnant. When he calls from the juvenile detention center. When you discover she is still cutting herself. When he says he wants nothing to do with your God. When she has run away. When the hospital calls to say he has overdosed.

You feel helpless. And hopeless.

But hold on. We have hope. Our God has said His name is Hope: "May the **God of hope** fill you with all joy and peace as you trust in him, so that you may overflow with hope by the power of the Holy Spirit" (Romans 15:13, emphasis added).

Why is that such good news? Why does it fill us with hope?

"[Even] if we are faithless, he will remain faithful, for he cannot disown himself" (2 Timothy 2:13, brackets mine).

He cannot disown or deny himself! God assures us that He *must* be true to who He is. His many names give an extensive picture of who He is and what He is like: Love, Peace, Almighty, Healer, Provider, Fortress, Defender . . .

. . . and Hope!

The meaning of hope—the desire of some good with expectation of obtaining it—is itself so hopeful. The acrostic below is helpful for remaining hopeful, even when we see no reason to hope:

Holding
On (with)
Patient
Expectation

When we hope, we acknowledge that we have not seen the answer we desire yet. Sometimes we don't even know what the answer is.

But we know the why and where and who of Hope: our faithful God. We can go to Him with our tears, fears, anger, despair—and He will give us hope.

That's it? Hope? No answers? We don't get what we are asking for? Our prodigals don't return, change, make better choices, follow Jesus?

Paul reminds us: "But hope that is seen is no hope at all. Who hopes for what they already have? But if we hope for what we do not yet have, we wait for it patiently" (Romans 8:24–25).

So we wait—and hope—with this assurance: "I am the LORD; in its time I will do this swiftly" (Isaiah 60:22).

RESPONSE:

1. How could knowing that one of God's names is Hope sustain you in your prayers?
2. How have you found it possible to feel helpless because you don't see a solution, yet to remain hopeful because of what you know about God?

DAY 71: 10 Reasons to Keep Hoping

It feels like we live on a battlefield, doesn't it? Like we have a relentless enemy, pursuing us and our loved prodigals. It seems, too often, every step in a good direction is followed by two in the wrong direction.

It feels that way because we *do* have an enemy, and he is determined to capture our wayward ones and take us down: "Be alert and of sober mind. Your enemy the devil prowls around like a roaring lion looking for someone to devour" (1 Peter 5:8).

But it's not hopeless.

Our God has given us many promises that we can keep hoping even as we fight for our loved ones on our knees. These ten assurances from God will lift you above the battlefield to see that He is with you and working for your prodigal.

1. **God is on our side:** "If God is for us, who can be against us?" (Romans 8:31).
2. **God holds us and our loved ones tightly:** "I give them eternal life, and they shall never perish; no one will snatch them out of my hand" (John 10:28).
3. **God never abandons us:** "The LORD himself goes before you and will be with you; he will never leave you nor forsake you. Do not be afraid; do not be discouraged" (Deuteronomy 31:8).
4. **God fights for us:** "So do not fear, for I am with you; do not be dismayed, for I am your God. I will strengthen you and help you; I will uphold you with my righteous right hand" (Isaiah 41:10).
5. **God hears and answers:** "I sought the LORD, and He answered me; He delivered me from all my fears" (Psalm 34:4).
6. **God's love is unfailing and forever:** "For I am convinced that neither death nor life, neither angels nor demons, neither the present nor the future, nor any powers, neither height nor depth, nor anything else in all creation, will be able to separate us from the love of God that is in Christ Jesus our Lord" (Romans 8:38–39).
7. **God is always with us:** "God has said, 'Never will I leave you; never will I forsake you'" (Hebrews 13:5).
8. **God is still working:** "Being confident of this, that he who began a good work in you will carry it on to completion until the day of Christ Jesus" (Philippians 1:6).
9. **God gives new hearts:** "I will give them an undivided heart and put a new spirit in them; I will remove from them their

heart of stone and give them a heart of flesh. Then they will follow my decrees and be careful to keep my laws. They will be my people, and I will be their God" (Ezekiel 11:19–20).

10. **God's goodness will prevail:** "I remain confident of this: I will see the goodness of the LORD in the land of the living. Wait for the LORD; be strong and take heart and wait for the LORD" (Psalm 27:13–14).

Even in the darkest days or in the fiercest battles, our God is there with us, strengthening us, sustaining us. And, equally, He is there for our loved ones, pursuing, wooing, reminding, loving them to himself.

Keep hoping.

RESPONSE:

1. What does today's battle for your loved one look like?
2. Which of these reasons for hope encouraged you the most? How?

DAY 72: Don't Despair

An ancient psalmist wrote, "Why, my soul, are you downcast? Why so disturbed within me?" (Psalm 42:5).

I've been there. I imagine you have as well—perhaps you are there even today.

Sometimes the frustration is fierce, the disappointment deep, the fear palpable, and the despair pervasive.

And hope? It has fled.

Somehow, in the midst of such desperation and hopelessness, the psalmist was able to say to his troubled soul, "Put your hope in God, for I will yet praise him, my Savior and my God" (Psalm 42:5).

How could he do that? How could he praise and hope?
I imagine he recalled the myriad promises from our God that
assure us of who He is and what He is like. Such as this song
of lament and praise:

> Because of the LORD's great love we are not consumed,
>   for his compassions never fail.
> They are new every morning;
>   great is your faithfulness.
> I say to myself, "The LORD is my portion;
>   therefore I will wait for him."
>
> The LORD is good to those whose hope is in him,
>   to the one who seeks him;
> it is good to wait quietly
>   for the salvation of the LORD. . . .
>
> Let him bury his face in the dust—
>   there may yet be hope.
>
> Lamentations 3:22–26, 29

And these words from the prophet Jeremiah:

> Restrain your voice from weeping and your eyes from
>   tears, for your work will be rewarded. . . .
> They will return from the land of the enemy.
> So there is hope for your descendants. . . . Your children
>   will return to their own land.
>
> Jeremiah 31:16–17

And perhaps this word to Israel:

> Return, Israel, to the LORD your God.
>   Your sins have been your downfall!
> Take words with you
>   and return to the LORD.
> Say to him:
>   "Forgive all our sins
> and receive us graciously,
>   that we may offer the fruit of our lips." . . .

> "I will heal their waywardness
>   and love them freely,
>   for my anger has turned away from them.
> I will be like the dew to Israel;
>   he will blossom like a lily."

Hosea 14:1–2, 4–5

And finally see how the psalmist received these promises from God:

> But the eyes of the LORD are on those who fear him,
>   on those whose hope is in his unfailing love,
> to deliver them from death
>   and keep them alive in famine.
> We wait in hope for the LORD;
>   he is our help and our shield.
> In him our hearts rejoice,
>   for we trust in his holy name.
> May your unfailing love be with us, LORD,
>   even as we put our hope in you.

Psalm 33:18–22

So perhaps the next time life with our prodigals causes us to cry out, "Why, my soul, are you downcast? Why so disturbed within me?" you and I will be able to see God's faithfulness to His people and the promise of hope He repeatedly gives. And we will be able to fall on our faces before the Lord, affirming that we can put our hope in God, saying, "I will yet praise him, my Savior and my God" (Psalm 42:5).

RESPONSE:

1. Is this season of your life touched more by despair or by hope? Describe.
2. What is one promise from the Word that lessens your despair and awakens hope?

DAY 73: Door of Hope

> I will make the Valley of Trouble a door of hope.
>
> Hosea 2:15 NCV

You may know the story of Hosea. God asked him to be a living symbol of His faithfulness to unfaithful Israel. So Hosea married a prostitute, loved her, gave her children—and pursued her when she returned to her former life.

God did the same to Israel—pursued her time and again when she turned from Him.

And that is what He does for our loved ones who have gone astray.

They have chosen a path that leads to the Valley of Trouble. They experience the consequences of their own choices. And they enter into danger they don't comprehend.

We therefore live with fear of what might happen to them. As their choices lead them deeper and deeper into the Valley of Trouble, our fears lead us deeper and deeper into hopelessness.

But God tells us: *Do not despair. I will make the Valley of Trouble a door of hope.*

God himself will meet them in that valley. He will open their eyes to see the depths of their pain and futility and danger. And He will open a door of hope to them—and lead them back into the light.

Of course, we don't know when He will open that door. But we know He is true to His names, and remember, one of His names is Hope: "May the God of hope fill you with all joy and peace as you trust in him, so that you may overflow with hope by the power of the Holy Spirit" (Romans 15:13).

May God fill you with Hope, even in the Valley of Trouble.

RESPONSE:

1. What does your prodigal's Valley of Trouble look like?
2. Will you trust God to turn it into a door of hope? Why or why not?

DAY 74: Hope as an Anchor

Josh married again five years ago, and he and his wife, Lesley, love to fish. Before they moved to their little farm, they owned a small boat and spent many hours in the ocean off Cocoa Beach and in the shipping channel running by a substantial rock jetty. The fish were usually biting by the jetty.

So they would pick a spot near the jetty, on the edge of the channel, and drop anchor. They would fish for hours . . . unless, of course, the anchor didn't hold, which happened occasionally.

Josh describes what they had to do: "I had to drop my pole—hopefully in the boat—run up to the front and start pulling in the anchor. Lesley would quickly start the engine and turn us away from the jetty—or we could have a big hole in the hull."

When his anchor didn't hold, it could have been disastrous.

But we have an anchor that will hold: "We have this hope as an anchor for the soul, firm and secure. It enters the inner sanctuary behind the curtain, where our forerunner, Jesus, has entered on our behalf" (Hebrews 6:19–20).

We have a tendency to place our hope in our prodigals—that they will come to their senses, repent, return, be restored. And they may, but not because they are a dependable anchor. Most of us have seen returned prodigals relapse or turn back to old friends and former patterns.

An anchor that will hold must be able to hold to any kind of undersea terrain and be strong enough to resist the wind and waves and currents.

We have that kind of anchor—God himself, revealed in Jesus: "I say to myself, 'The LORD is my portion; therefore I will wait for him'" (Lamentations 3:24).

Hear God's Word for you in Isaiah 49:23: "Then you will know that I am the LORD; those who hope in me will not be disappointed."

Receive the prayer of Paul in Ephesians 1:18–19: "I pray that the eyes of your heart may be enlightened in order that you may know the hope to which he has called you, the riches of his glorious inheritance in his holy people, and his incomparably great power for us who believe."

As we enter into the war room on behalf of our prodigals, as we accept God's invitation to come to His throne of grace, we can do so with confidence that our Hope will hold. Jesus is the anchor who is solid and dependable.

When we pray for our prodigals, we pour out our heart's desires. We cry out to our God. We beseech Him to woo and win, to rescue and restore. We ask Him to lavish them with love, immerse them in mercy, and embrace them with grace.

We know that the God of Hope is our anchor, and that our anchor will hold.

We join with Micah in proclaiming, "But as for me, I watch in hope for the Lord, I wait for God my Savior; my God will hear me" (Micah 7:7).

As much as we pray for, give mercy to, persevere on behalf of, and never give up on our loved prodigals—and do so much more in pursuing redemption, restoration, reconciliation, and relationship with them—so much infinitely more does *God* do all those for *us*, and for our loved ones.

Thus we can hope.

RESPONSE:

1. What anchors have you tried to rely on and seen them fail you?

2. When has hope in God been your anchor, the force that firmly secures you?

9

SPIRIT

"Not by might nor by power, but by my Spirit," says the LORD Almighty.

Zechariah 4:6

No matter what human influence, pressure, or leverage we think we may have to bring about change within the prodigals we love, God always reminds us that real change comes through the action of His own Spirit.

All that we have considered in these pages to help us walk through our prodigal wilderness is impossible for us alone. But the Holy Spirit makes it possible.

The Holy Spirit is the secret for living the Christian life. Jesus said it was better for Him to leave so the Spirit could come to live in us. Amazingly, we become the home of God himself as His Spirit comes to dwell in us. And oh! What amazing things He does for us.

In His Word, we find His very present Spirit is our Advocate, Comforter, Encourager, Truth, Freedom, Peace, Warrior, and our Power. In chapter 5, "Trust," we looked at many of these marvelous roles from the angle of learning to trust Him more. This time, let's lean in even further. What are the ways in which the Holy Spirit supports and sustains us?

DAY 75: Advocate

As a writer, I sometimes receive requests to endorse books—most often from friends. They want me to vouch for them, to say their book is well written and worthy of reading. In a sense, my friends are asking me to be an advocate for them.

Certainly those of us who love prodigals understand this advocate role. How many times have we spoken for or on behalf of our wayward ones: in their schools, in the courts, for a job, even to our friends?

Yes, we desire and encourage appropriate consequences for their choices. Yet our love compels us to be on their side—an ally. To believe in and endorse them. To be an advocate for them.

Gratefully, God has provided an Advocate for us and for our loved ones: "But the Advocate, the Holy Spirit, whom the Father will send in my name, will teach you everything, and remind you of all that I have said to you" (John 14:26 NRSV).

The New Testament Greek word for Holy Spirit is *parakletos*. In most recent translations, the meaning given is "advocate." An advocate is one who speaks for or on behalf of, or speaks up for, to give a character reference for someone.

How often do we feel inadequate and unworthy to come to the Father with our desperate needs as parents and family and friends? Yet the Holy Spirit is there. He speaks to the Father on our behalf because of what Jesus has done for us. He offers a character reference for us—*the character of Jesus himself.*

He is also an advocate for our prodigals. He brings to God's attention the fact that He shed His blood for these we love, that there are children of God on their knees pleading on behalf of these prodigals.

And this Holy Advocate does something else: He actually prays for us and for them. "In the same way, the Spirit helps us in our weakness. We do not know what we ought to pray for, but the Spirit himself intercedes for us through wordless groans" (Romans 8:26).

His prayers go much deeper, with infinite understanding. What a comfort!

As we pray for our loved prodigals, we can be assured that the Holy Spirit, our Advocate, is standing with us, speaking for us, praying for us.

RESPONSE:

1. The Holy Spirit is not only our Advocate (before the Father as well as against Satan's accusations), but He is our prodigals' Advocate as well. Is there an aspect of these truths that you find hard to accept? Why?

2. What do you think the Holy Spirit says when He prays for you? For your prodigal?

DAY 76: Comforter

As we read, the word Jesus used when introducing the Holy Spirit is *parakletos*. It is a rich word with multiple meanings or connotations. In addition to "advocate," another way the word is translated, most often in older versions, is *comforter*.

In the midst of the pain of walking through life with a loved prodigal, one of the best gifts we receive is someone who comes alongside us and walks with us, to comfort and console.

Hopefully most of us have a friend who does that for us.

But we have this assurance: God is that friend. He has sent us *parakletos*, who is called beside to comfort us—to soothe and reassure us:

"And I will pray the Father, and he shall give you another Comforter, that he may abide with you for ever" (John 14:16 KJV).

Thus, as we live through the often difficult days with a loved one, God himself, by His Spirit, comes alongside us to comfort and console us. What a promise and provision!

And as we walk beside our prodigals, or friends going through such a trial, we can receive comfort and also be the conduit through whom the Spirit can offer comfort and consolation: "who comforts us in all our troubles, so that we can comfort those in any trouble with the comfort we ourselves receive from God" (2 Corinthians 1:4).

When our Josh had received Christ, and that night had been born in my heart as my son, I entered into one of the most challenging times of our wilderness journey.

He was in the Christian residential program God had provided, but we could see him only once a week. My heart ached. I wept. No one really understood!

Except for the Holy Spirit, who comforted me and walked through those weeks with me.

RESPONSE:

1. Describe a time when comfort was exactly what you needed and the Holy Spirit provided it.

2. How have you been a conduit of comfort in another's life?

DAY 77: Encourager

This amazing word *parakletos* offers even more.

How often do you find yourself saying:

"Can I confront him one more time?"

"Will I stand firm on the consequences we outlined?"

"Can I go through with the intervention?"

"I need more courage than I have."

I have treasured those who encouraged me during the darkest, most challenging days of life with a prodigal. They listened, they shared from their experience, they reminded me of truths from God's Word that encouraged me.

That is one of the things the Holy Spirit does for us—He encourages us.

The important thing to see in this word is the meaning of *encourage*: to en-courage, that is, to put courage into. One of the roles the Holy Spirit plays in our lives is to instill in us the courage we need for the moment as well as for the journey.

Ezra, a priest and teacher during the end of the Babylonian captivity, had been appointed by God and the pagan king of the Persian Empire to go to Jerusalem to teach the returned exiles God's laws and to help reestablish the Temple worship.

Though he had the full backing of the imperial government, Ezra had no idea how he would be received by the fellow Israelites he had to face. Many had been born in Babylon and knew nothing of God's law. Many had been exposed to the idols and customs of Babylon. Would they be calloused, rebellious, self-absorbed, and sold out to the pagan world?

Ezra needed courage. He needed the Encourager.

He wrote, "Because the hand of the LORD my God was on me, I took courage and gathered leaders from Israel to go up with me" (Ezra 7:28).

Note that he took courage. It was there, in the Lord, for the taking, and he helped himself to it.

When the Holy Spirit came at Pentecost, the 120 disciples were filled with the Encourager. They began to do and say things they had never been able to do or say before. They even had courage to withstand a trial and speak out about Jesus Christ.

Luke reported: "When they saw the courage of Peter and John and realized that they were unschooled, ordinary men, they were astonished and they took note that these men had been with Jesus" (Acts 4:13).

Later, after they were warned, threatened, and released, they returned to the other believers and together they prayed: "Now, Lord, consider their threats and enable your servants to speak your word with great boldness [courage]" (Acts 4:29, brackets mine).

We can ask the Spirit to give us courage to stand firm, to make hard choices, to keep loving unconditionally.

And we can ask the Spirit to give our loved ones courage to turn from the path they are on, to withdraw from friends who mislead them, to get help, to repent, and to surrender to our loving Father.

I am so grateful our Father has provided for us in every challenge of this wilderness journey.

RESPONSE:

1. When was the last time you desperately needed courage?
2. In what ways does your prodigal need courage right now? How can you be praying for him or her?

DAY 78: Truth

Lies.

One of the realities of living with and loving prodigals is lies.

How many times have you heard, "Why don't you trust me?" Or, "You can trust me."

If our prodigal is an adolescent, a driver's license opens the door for deception. We don't really know where they are going or what they are doing.

If our prodigal is using or abusing drugs, we can be sure of one thing: If he is saying something, he is probably lying.

They become masters of partial truth, deception, manipulation. They lie to our faces with utmost conviction.

They are not the only liars.

We lie to ourselves. We deny the severity of their addictions. We are sure our good training will cause them to make good choices. We choose to accept their explanations rather than face unwelcome facts.

We believe what they say they are doing, who they are with. We bail them out of jail, certain that they will be grateful and change.

And there is another liar, the father of lies: Satan assures us we can trust our prodigal.

Then, after trust is broken, he accuses us of being terrible parents, telling us that their waywardness is all our fault. He bombards us with hopeless scenarios: Our loved one will never change. She or he is gone. The rest of our lives will be misery.

But there is the one who speaks truth: the Spirit of Truth.

In John 14:16 and 15:26, Jesus assures us this Spirit of truth will live in us. And we also have this wonderful promise: "But when he, the Spirit of truth, comes, he will guide you into all the truth" (John 16:13).

He will speak truth to us and through us. He can also give us discernment regarding what our prodigals tell us. We can even know things directly from the Spirit that enable us to intervene or rescue.

Our son was a prodigal in the early days of kids on the internet. I would check his computer often to see where he had been. He would change his password, but every time, the Spirit would tell me the new password.

The Spirit will reveal to us the lies we tell ourselves and enable us to walk in truth. The Spirit will confound the lies of the devil with the truth of God.

Imagine! We have God's Spirit of all truth, living in us, teaching us, guiding us. So it makes sense to be filling our minds with the truth of God's Word, giving the Spirit of truth all He needs to renew our minds and change our lives.

And we can pray the same for our prodigals.

RESPONSE:

1. In what area of untruth do you find yourself struggling most: your prodigal's lies, your lies to yourself, Satan's lies that there is no problem, or Satan's lies that the situation is hopeless?

2. What truth do you think the Holy Spirit wants to impress on you right now to help end that struggle?

DAY 79: Freedom

Imprisoned. Trapped. No way out!

Josh was high on pain medication after having his wisdom teeth removed. When he headed to his car to leave, his dad intervened—Josh wasn't safe to drive.

Josh said he could go if he wanted, but when his dad stepped between him and his car, he ran into the house and called 9-1-1 to report that someone was about to get hurt. He returned with a hammer in his hand and approached his dad at the car.

A friend tried to intervene, the police arrived, Josh ran, but they caught him. Two nights in juvenile detention, a court appearance, and several weeks at a boys' facility assured him that he preferred freedom.

This story could be true for many of our prodigals. Some are in jail. Others live in addictions. Many are in deep financial trouble. Their choices have created cords that bind and bars that restrain.

All too often those same choices have the same effect on us. We feel imprisoned and bound as well. And if the actions of our loved ones don't entrap us, then the enemy of our souls will do the entrapping with his clever schemes. He will accuse us of causing the problems. He will assault us with guilt and hopelessness.

But we don't have to live in bondage. We have a spirit—the Holy Spirit—who liberates us: "Now the Lord is the Spirit, and where the Spirit of the Lord is, there is freedom" (2 Corinthians 3:17).

As we allow Him to fill us and control us, as we rest in Him instead of striving in our own efforts, He will loose the cords and break the bars.

We can't do it ourselves—it is impossible for us. But nothing is impossible for our God, through the power of His Holy Spirit. If we surrender to Him, He will free our minds from despair and our hearts from fear. He will give peace and rest.

He is also the one who can bring freedom to our lost ones.

RESPONSE:

1. In what way do you allow yourself to be imprisoned by your thoughts about your loved prodigal, and how you deal with him/her?
2. How might the Holy Spirit be breaking through that prison to reestablish you in the freedom that He promises?

DAY 80: Peace

The chaos was almost palpable.

Josh and his friends barged through the front door. The kitchen was the first stop, then they scaled the stairs to his room in a few leaps.

In the early years it was just boy noise and roughhousing. But as the years went on, it escalated. We wanted him and his friends to feel welcome in our home, but their boyishness became abusive—to our home, to our values, to our peace.

Peace.

I remember peace in our home—when our children were young and responsive. When I didn't have to hide my purse from his friends. When I didn't need a man to stay there when we were gone just to protect our home.

I remember peace in my heart—before Josh had a car and I knew where he was. Before he had a computer and I didn't have to worry about what he was exploring. Before his activities became risky, even dangerous and destructive.

Gratefully, Jesus promised us peace repeatedly: "Peace I leave with you; my peace I give you. I do not give to you as the world gives. Do not let your hearts be troubled and do not be afraid" (John 14:27).

"I have told you these things, so that in me you may have peace. In this world you will have trouble. But take heart! I have overcome the world" (John 16:33).

The Apostle Paul also assured us of peace: "And the peace of God, which transcends all understanding, will guard your hearts and your minds in Christ Jesus" (Philippians 4:7).

Remember the source of peace.

In the first verse above, the peace Jesus offers comes from the Spirit, as indicated in the verse that precedes it: "But the Advocate, the Holy Spirit, whom the Father will send in my name, will teach you everything, and remind you of all I have said to you. Peace I leave with you; my peace I give to you" (John 14:26–27 NRSV).

Paul also makes clear the source of our peace:

- "The mind governed by the flesh is death, but the mind governed by the Spirit is life and peace" (Romans 8:6).
- "For the kingdom of God is not a matter of eating and drinking, but of righteousness, peace and joy in the Holy Spirit" (Romans 14:17).
- "But the fruit of the Spirit is love, joy, peace, forbearance, kindness, goodness, faithfulness, gentleness and self-control" (Galatians 5:22–23).

Thus, when your prodigal and his or her choices bring turmoil, anxiety, worry, or fear, you can ask the Spirit for the peace that passes all understanding.

RESPONSE:

1. Reread the Scriptures shared about peace. Which one is most meaningful to you right now? Why?

2. Are you finding that it is possible to live in a state of alertness and discernment regarding your prodigal, but also be experiencing God's peace? If not, what can you pray today to bring you to that point? What can you pray each day to help you remain there?

DAY 81: Warrior

In chapter 1, "Love," I shared a story to show how love goes to war for a loved one. It was about the night our prodigal came to Christ, when two additional, greatly significant events occurred.

I want to revisit those events to underline the magnificent truth that the Holy Spirit is our Warrior.

First, I had a vision in which God poured His love for Josh into me, assuring me I would need it. Yes, I have needed it.

Second, that began three sleepless nights engaged in fierce battle with the powers and principalities of the prince of the air—the devil himself.

My understanding was that the evil one had always assumed this boy was his. His heritage and early life put him undeniably in Satan's domain. So when prayers were answered and he said yes to Jesus, the devil was not happy.

Perhaps the devil thought if he could defeat me he would regain control over our son. If I had been battling on my own, I would surely have lost. But no. I had a far more powerful Warrior on my side—the Spirit himself.

He was my defense—and also this boy's defense, shielding us from the fiery darts sent our way. And He was on the attack, giving me words of truth, courage, fearlessness, wisdom—whatever I needed in the battle.

That part of the battle lasted for three nights, and then I was given rest. But the conflict continued.

Many tears and fears revealed my weakness, but unceasing prayer and supernatural strength and wisdom from the Spirit enabled me to stand in the gap for my son. And He still enables me, for our enemy is relentless.

The Holy Spirit was and is always with me and in me. He was the Warrior I needed in this ongoing spiritual war. And as He fought for and through me, He was also the Warrior my son needed. And He still is.

You, too, are in a battle, as is the prodigal you love and pray for.

Unfortunately, we too often try to win the war on our own. We forget that we are completely outmatched—in the struggle for our loved ones and in all the other ways the evil one seeks to defeat us and our wanderers.

We cannot do it alone.

Gratefully, our loving Father and beloved Savior have sent the Spirit to be in us and with us. To fight beside us, for us, through us—and He is far greater than our enemy.

See what He promises us:

- "You are from God, little children, and have overcome them; because greater is He who is in you than he who is in the world" (1 John 4:4 NASB).
- "This is what the LORD says to you: 'Do not be afraid or discouraged because of this vast army. For the battle is not yours, but God's'" (2 Chronicles 20:15).

- "'Not by might nor by power, but by My Spirit,' says the LORD of hosts" (Zechariah 4:6 NASB).

It's important to remember that we face a defeated but still powerful enemy, and we are still in the battle.

God himself has provided for us the required armor, which I have pointed out several times. We just need to remember to wear it.

Put on the full armor of God, so that you can take your stand against the devil's schemes. For our struggle is not against flesh and blood, but against the rulers, against the authorities, against the powers of this dark world and against the spiritual forces of evil in the heavenly realms.

Therefore put on the full armor of God, so that when the day of evil comes, you may be able to stand your ground, and after you have done everything, to stand.

Stand firm then, with the belt of truth buckled around your waist, with the breastplate of righteousness in place, and with your feet fitted with the readiness that comes from the gospel of peace.

In addition to all this, take up the shield of faith, with which you can extinguish all the flaming arrows of the evil one.

Take the helmet of salvation and the sword of the Spirit, which is the word of God.

And pray in the Spirit on all occasions with all kinds of prayers and requests.

Ephesians 6:11–18

What does God give us for this battle?

These are our weapons: truth, righteousness, peace, faith, salvation, the Word of God, prayer. Not our own strength or wisdom, not anger or retribution or revenge, not our cleverness nor our power.

And most important, He gives us His Spirit, a Warrior to fight for us in the battle for the souls of our loved ones.

RESPONSE:

1. Ponder the idea of the gracious, gentle, and peace-giving Spirit as a Warrior—your Warrior! What thoughts come to mind?
2. Pray through the passage in Ephesians about the armor of God. Which weapon or piece of protection do you need the most today? Why?

DAY 82: Power

How many times did I say to the Lord, "You think I am stronger than I am. I am too weak. I can't do this!"

Do what? Keep going. Listen to one more lie. Lower my voice. Find an effective consequence. Meet with the principal one more time. Get yelled at again. Love unconditionally. Maintain hope.

God's response always runs something like this: *Actually, Judy, you don't know how totally weak you are. No, you can't do "this." In fact, you can't do anything. Dealing with, helping, surviving your prodigal is impossible for you.*

Fortunately, He always adds: *Of course, all things are possible for me. I have not left you to do this on your own. I have sent my Spirit to empower you, to make you strong enough for "this" and anything else.*

Just look at these assurances of all the power we need. You will recognize some of these potent truths from previous chapters:

Power from Him, not from ourselves: "'Not by might nor by power, but by My Spirit,' says the LORD of hosts" (Zechariah 4:6 NASB).

Power to be witnesses and speak truth for Him: "But you will receive power when the Holy Spirit comes on you; and you will be my witnesses" (Acts 1:8).

Power to live in joy, peace, and hope: "May the God of hope fill you with all joy and peace as you trust in him, so that you may overflow with hope by the power of the Holy Spirit" (Romans 15:13).

Power to live out love and courage: "For the Spirit God gave us does not make us timid, but gives us power, love and self-discipline" (2 Timothy 1:7).

Power that enters our weakness and makes us strong: "But he said to me, 'My grace is sufficient for you, for my power is made perfect in weakness.' Therefore I will boast all the more gladly about my weaknesses, so that Christ's power may rest on me" (2 Corinthians 12:9).

Power to strengthen us from the inside: "I pray that out of his glorious riches he may strengthen you with power through his Spirit in your inner being" (Ephesians 3:16).

Power for endurance and patience: "Being strengthened with all power according to his glorious might so that you may have great endurance and patience" (Colossians 1:11).

Power to receive answers to your prayers: "The prayer of a righteous person is powerful and effective" (James 5:16).

Power for everything we need: "His divine power has given us everything we need for a godly life through our knowledge of him who called us by his own glory and goodness" (2 Peter 1:3).

Power beyond what we can ask or imagine: "Now to him who is able to do immeasurably more than all we ask or imagine, according to his power that is at work within us" (Ephesians 3:20).

So if we need power to speak truth, make hard decisions, forgive, love unconditionally, to leave them in jail—or just to keep going—God's Spirit, living in us, is able and available to give us all the power we need, even more than we know we need.

RESPONSE:

1. Think of a time when God's power enabled you to do something you used to think was impossible. How has that built your trust in God's available power for current challenges?

2. Which of the aspects of the Holy Spirit's power listed above do you need right now? How will you access that power today?

10

GIFT

Thank God for this gift too wonderful for words!

2 Corinthians 9:15 NLT

Gifts in the wilderness?

You don't expect to find one of your best gifts ever when you are wandering through the wilderness. A walk in the wilderness might be lovely if you're a nature lover and you keep your eyes open. You could discover some real gems: colorful creatures, spectacular plants, encounters with startling animals, an astounding array of colors and shapes underwater, hidden waterfalls.

But a walk in the wilderness could also be frightening and full of surprises that turn out to be dangerous. This is the wilderness we know as lovers of prodigals.

Along the way you will experience fear, anger, frustration, doubt, desperation, hopelessness. You encounter people and situations you would never have known, nor want to know. Every way you try to help him or her toward a safe and productive life fails, and you often feel like a failure.

But if you keep your eyes—and your mind and heart—open, you will discover treasures you never anticipated. Loving a prodigal can introduce you to deep needs in hurting people, broken families and broken systems, a depth of empathy and compassion you have never felt before, and opportunities to offer comfort and love.

Loving a prodigal will also open doors of understanding and tenderness toward the wanderer you love—if you will open your ears, pay attention, and listen. It will help you learn life lessons you have hoped your prodigal will grasp. You will be able to recognize old patterns of relating and communicating, and adopt new approaches that will transform your future with your loved one.

There's more. In this chapter we will be wilderness explorers, discovering eight invaluable gifts to transform your life. By the time we are done, you may find yourself on your knees in gratitude to God.

And the best gift you will find in this wilderness journey will be your prodigal. He or she will be the channel through which God does a beautiful work in you. And you will lay the groundwork for a rich, new relationship with your prodigal someday to come.

DAY 83: A Gift of Mercy

What was the last thing your prodigal did that really exasperated you?

Lied to you? Stole from you? Drove high or intoxicated? Moved in with a girlfriend/boyfriend? Refused to go to school? Did something foolish and dangerous?

What was your response?

What was the last thing you did that might have saddened God?

Probably not the obviously destructive things your prodigal might have done. But God is saddened by many of our choices in response to our loved ones or to other events and circumstances in our lives: anger, hurtful words, harsh punishments, fear, deceit, lack of kindness or compassion, unloving attitude, impatience. It could be a long list.

And what was God's response? Think of Jesus' responses to people in Scripture, such as the woman at the well or the thief on the cross (see chapter 2, "Grace").

And then there's the woman who was caught in adultery. The story is in John 8:1–11. The woman's accusers surely had set up the "caught in the act" shaming of this woman. Dragged from bed, apparently, and thrust at the feet of Jesus, she awaited His condemnation—and her own death. "Let any one of you who is without sin be the first to throw a stone at her."

She cringed, anticipating. She heard nothing but the sound of stones dropping to the ground and feet shuffling away.

"Woman, where are they? Has no one condemned you?"

"No one, sir," the amazed woman replied.

"Then neither do I condemn you," Jesus declared. "Go now and leave your life of sin."

Jesus showed mercy to her, and she hadn't even cried out for it.

And you and I? Surely we too often find ourselves crying out to God for mercy as David did after his sin with Bathsheba: "Have mercy on me, O God, according to your unfailing love; according to your great compassion blot out my transgressions" (Psalm 51:1).

We are grateful our God is like the merciful father in Luke 15: As the father's prodigal wanderer returned, before he could even speak his repentance, the father ran to him, threw his arms around him, kissed him, put a cloak and a ring on him, and threw a party.

Our God loves mercy. One of Josh's great gifts to me is grasping that truth. Our God is willing to immerse us in His mercy: "But because of his great love for us, God, who is rich in mercy, made us alive with Christ even when we were dead in transgressions—it is by grace you have been saved" (Ephesians 2:4–5).

Yes, God is opposed to sin. And sin generates consequences—some that are the natural result of choices made, others that we impose.

But our primary response should be one that flows out of the love and grace we ourselves have received. Even as we have been immersed in the mercy of our God, so should we give mercy to our prodigals.

We should be less like the Pharisees dragging in the woman caught in adultery and more like the very-wronged father who ran to his prodigal son.

May we live in this truth: "Mercy triumphs over judgment" (James 2:13).

RESPONSE:

1. When has mercy been given to you?
2. How consistent are you at extending mercy to your prodigal? Explain.

DAY 84: A Gift of Grace

Grace was not a word from my early life. I wanted my own way and pursued it relentlessly. I wasn't usually mean, but I didn't know what grace was.

When I met Jesus in high school, I began to get a glimpse of grace. After all, I was saved by grace through faith. And that began a journey of growing in grace.

Looking back over the years, I see how the grace of God protected me from some wrong choices: He extracted me from the wrong crowd in high school. He said if I married the good man I was engaged to, I wouldn't be able to do what He wanted me to do. I began to recognize evidences of grace.

I remember sitting by the pool at Arrowhead Springs in California, looking out over the valley, asking, "Why me, God? Why am I so blessed, so privileged?" Another hint at grace.

And the work God called me to: living my dream to be a magazine writer and editor—for Him! The amazing privilege of working with (Cru founder) Bill Bright! Meeting humble servants of God, writing about what God was doing in people's lives all over the globe. So much grace.

It didn't feel like grace when I waited and waited, through five years of dating, for Steve Douglass to decide he should get married. But when he proposed to me, I was overcome with God's grace to give me such a man.

Children are great grace instructors. It took a lot of grace to make it through my first daughter's first months—a hurting tummy and constant tears. Daughter number two slept much of her first year— a kind grace from the Lord. And they both have been grace to me throughout their lives.

One of my greatest teachers? Our son, Josh.

Oh, the grace.

God gave grace to this boy to lift him out of his unstable situation into a home where he received love and security and many advantages.

It took His grace to give me the *understanding* of His grace! I needed to go much deeper into grasping how God has shed His grace on me.

Grace to endure and persevere through Josh's wilderness journey.

Grace for me to give, extend, repeat, offer, sometimes grudgingly, sometimes through tears, but increasingly freely and joyfully—grace.

As is true for all of us, comprehending something of the grace of God takes a journey—sometimes a long one. God didn't give up on me—He kept pouring it on, opening my eyes and heart to see grace, and even showed me how to give grace to others.

The grace to give and to receive that I learned from Josh has been extended broadly and deeply to family, friends, co-workers, and strangers. I understand more each day that God calls us to be His arms of grace to all those we encounter.

And yes, to me. Oh, the grace He keeps giving.

RESPONSE:

1. How have you seen grace in your life through loving your prodigal?
2. Where have you given unexpected grace?

DAY 85: A Gift of Prayer

I used to think I knew how to pray. Then this wilderness journey with my wandering son required desperate prayer.

And I moved into a new dimension of what it meant to pray.

Even now I realize I still know so little about praying. Prayer is a wonder I can barely comprehend. Sometimes I feel woefully inadequate and terribly ineffective—does anything happen when I pray?

Yet I pray.

Often. Always.

Here are some of the ways I pray. This is not a formula. There is no order, because life in the moment dictates how I come to the Lord, what I say, what position I'm in.

We'll start with one of my favorite ways to pray: walking on the beach. An hour conversation with my God, with the sand in my toes, the waves lapping my ankles, the ocean masking nearby sounds. I usually ask, "What do you want to say to me?" But sometimes I start with, "I have something to say. . . ."

I almost always pray with great honesty. I find it's good to tell God the truth—He knows it anyway. The beach is a good place to yell out my anger or fear or confusion. My home, when no one else is there, also works. He always listens patiently and responds compassionately. Reminding me of truths I know, of what He is like, of how I need to respond.

Sometimes I fall on my face—literally—in awe that the God of the universe would invite me into His presence, to talk with Him, to share my heart, to listen to His. I am so unworthy, yet He treasures me and wants me with Him!

Or I might drop to my knees and cry out, begging God to choose to do what I know He can do. Would He please heal, or rescue, or provide, or change things? Change a mind or a heart or a situation? Jesus says He responds to those who cry out day and night. So I do.

Many times, as David describes in the Psalms, my tears have soaked my pillow. "Help me, Lord."

I pray by myself and with others. I pray through Scripture. I read aloud prayers written by others. I raise my hands in worship.

Of course, I have interceded on behalf of those I love, friends and co-workers, our leaders, world situations, those needing justice . . . and many other people, needs, events. And for those who love a prodigal.

I am grateful that one of my most frequent prayers is, "Thank you, Lord." I have taken seriously the admonition to give thanks in all things, and oh, the difference it has made in all the above prayers!

I thank Him. Do I thank Him because He has answered my prayer? Well yes, He answers, though sometimes my hearing is not so good. Often He says, "No, not a good idea." Other times He says yes, but it usually looks a little different from what I had in mind. Most often He says, "I have a better idea." So I thank Him for His answer—and just for listening.

He is always on time—with His great knowledge and love. As I shared several times in this book, my saying "Thank you" affirms that I believe He is God and He is good. And in my experience, those little words are like a key to open a door for God to work.

I've experienced some amazing answers to prayer. I've seen people healed in heart and body. I've enjoyed remarkable community praying with others.

Yes, sometimes God seems silent. At those times, I feel like I know nothing about praying. I grow weary of waiting.

Then, once again, my *Abba* Daddy invites me into His embrace, into His heart. We talk and listen and cry and laugh.

How sweet is that!

RESPONSE:

1. What are some ways you pray?
2. When have you found unexpected treasures in your praying?

DAY 86: A Gift of Love

In chapter 1, "Love," we talked about real love. I related this statement I received from God: *"By definition, unconditional love doesn't require love in return."*

I know it's true. God loved me first—long before I loved Him, when I was definitely living in my sins. And even after I responded to that love and accepted His gift of salvation, I haven't always loved Him well—you know, by obeying Him. But He has never quit loving me.

Parents learn this early. Even before a baby is born, they love her. And the moment they see her, they are "head over heels" in love. It's a good thing, because that baby demands everything and gives no love in return for quite a while.

Fortunately, they grow up and learn to love. Unfortunately, when they become teens, sometimes they break our hearts with words like "Leave me alone! I hate you!" or "You're not my real mother!"

Our son made it hard to love him.

Many of his actions were enough to eradicate all my love for him—but they didn't. I thought I was loving unconditionally.

He first came to us because his birth mother couldn't care for him, and he was hurt and confused. He couldn't call me Mom and he couldn't love me—that would be betraying his "real" mother.

As the years passed, I grew to love him deeply. But as he grew, he had much pain to work through. He made lots of negative choices. He was trying to figure out who he was, and loving me was not a priority. And sometimes that was painful to me.

I would ask God, "Would it be so hard for him to be able to say 'I love you' to me—just once?" The Lord responded so clearly: *"Judy, unconditional love doesn't require love in return."*

What a gift Josh gave me—helping me begin to understand the depth of God's love for me. If I never loved Him in return, or did what He asked me to do, or lived in a Christ-like manner, or even if

I committed a terrible crime, He would keep loving me. I couldn't *make* him quit loving me.

That's the kind of love—truly unconditional—God asked me to have for our son. So I kept loving him. No matter what.

I will never forget the day Josh said, "I love you." Those words came from a painful situation of his own. I was grateful that day and I am grateful even now when they come easily off his lips and are proven in his actions day after day.

And I thank God He used this boy—now a man—to teach me the real meaning of unconditional love.

RESPONSE:

1. When has it been challenging for you to keep loving your prodigal?
2. How could you apply unconditional love to the situation?

DAY 87: A Gift of Perseverance

I don't think I've ever asked for the gift of perseverance. I might desire persistence, fortitude, even patience or endurance, but not perseverance—it sounds so painful.

But that's a gift I received often. Especially during this prodigal journey. I wrote this in the midst of a hard time:

Never Give Up

Sometimes it seems to no avail.
You love unconditionally as best you can.
You apply some tough love.
You encourage, affirm, look for the good.
You set boundaries and enforce consequences.
You forgive and forgive and forgive again.
You pour out mercy and grace.

And they keep going their wayward way.
They reject you, disappear from your life.
Or even when they make better choices, they take you for
    granted.
The casual "Thanks" hardly conveys gratitude.
The offhand apology seems barely sincere.
Coming around again with outstretched hand.
Then gone until the next neediness.
You cry, you pray.
You reach out, you let go.
You wait.

Sound familiar?

I've had those thoughts, those questions. Wondering how it will end. When it will end.

Perhaps our God, our loving Father, could write something similar about *us*. Surely, occasionally, we have the same attitudes, responses, words, and actions toward Him that our beloved prodigals have toward us. Yet He keeps loving, correcting, encouraging . . .

He gives out extravagant mercy and grace.

He waits.

He perseveres.

And so can we, in His Spirit.

RESPONSE:

1. Could you have written this personal litany? With what lines do you especially connect?

2. How have you been able to persevere? How would you explain it to someone else?

DAY 88: A Gift of Surrender

I am a strong-willed, stubborn person. I have been from the beginning. Just ask my family.

When I came to Christ at age fifteen, I made a purposeful exchange: "God, I choose your way, not mine."

I thought it was settled. But by the next day, I discovered I would be making the choice—my way or God's way?—every day, sometimes many times a day.

And so it has been. Apparently my stubborn self-will is deeply ingrained. Many times God has waited patiently for me to open my hands to let go of my way. Sometimes He has had to apply a small crowbar to my clenched fists to precipitate surrender.

Loving a prodigal revealed the depth of my desire to have my own way. My appeals to God often demanded or cajoled or bartered. Surely He would intervene and rescue our son—and us—from this agonizing journey.

God listened and received my prayers with love and grace. Then He reminded me that He had a better way.

The children of Israel had a similar problem. They were stubborn and self-willed. In Isaiah 30 the Lord lays out a litany of their refusal to choose His way, of their ongoing rebellion, of their rejection of His plans.

Then He says these amazing words: "In repentance and rest you will be saved; in quietness and trust is your strength. But you were not willing" (Isaiah 30:15 NASB).

Not willing.

Yes, that applies to my rebellious loved one. But I believe in *this* case God is speaking to *me*.

I so often think I know what is best. I still want God to do it my way, what I think will be the less painful way. The easier way. I don't want to live with this pain. I don't want to lose my child. I want to be free from fear and anxiety and hopelessness. But I want to do it my way. My fingers are tightly clasped. Surrender seems unacceptable.

But my Father offers rest and repentance, quietness and strength—what I need for this journey.

Slowly I learn that God's way really is better than my way. He is patient and determined. He wants me to become the person He designed me to be. He wants me to be ready to do the good works He has prepared for me.

And just perhaps this loved prodigal who has taken me where I did not want to go, who has revealed my own stubbornness, is *the means by which God will accomplish His good purposes in me.*

Am I willing?

RESPONSE:

1. How has the gift of surrender—your surrender to God—eased your journey in the wilderness of loving a prodigal?
2. When did you realize that God's purposes for your prodigal were equally about you?

DAY 89: A Gift of Community

Much of my prodigal journey—and what you have read in this book—has occurred in kinship with the wonderful Prayer for Prodigals community.

We have shared our struggles and tears. We have rejoiced over small steps in a good direction and fallen on our knees as we have heard of backward movement, and sometimes even loss of life.

God has done wonderful grace work in our community—in each of us and in our prodigals. Clearly our first priority has been to pray for our loved ones to turn and to return—to God and to us. I'm so grateful for His faithfulness to us and to them in hearing and answering our prayers.

But I've glimpsed how much more God has been doing in us and through us. Let me try to capture the essence of four realities happening as I have participated in a praying community.

We have drawn near to God. In desperation we turn to Him with all our fears, laying our needs before Him, pouring out our hearts for our prodigals to Him. We have accepted His invitation to join Him at the throne of grace in prayer. We ask, we seek, we knock, we beg, we thank—and we keep on because He has said we can.

We recognize we are also prodigals. When we plead for our prodigals, we do so in humility, realizing we need rescuing as well. Much of our study in the Word—such as the chapters in this book—has been to hear from God what He is doing in us. This wilderness journey is a potent place for God to work and to accomplish His good plans in us.

Love and grace guide us. We've seen how He has dealt with us in such tenderness, loving us unconditionally, and pouring His grace over us time and again. He reminds us that love and grace are the strongest ways to draw our loved ones back. So, as we make hard choices and maintain clear boundaries and consequences, love and grace flow through our words, our actions, our arms.

We are doing the impossible. To endure the pain, to rise above the fear, to keep believing and hoping, to love unconditionally, to give grace and blessing instead of resentment and anger—these are impossible for us. So we receive the gracious enabling and empowering of God's Holy Spirit to carry us through.

I recognize that everyone who reads this book may not be part of a safe community. I would encourage you to take a brave step and open up with people you trust. Be vulnerable to share your pain and your fear. Invite them to pray for you and the one you love. And you are always welcome in the Prayer for Prodigals community. (See Resources on page 236.)

I am grateful to God for bringing our praying community together. We entrust our hearts and our prodigals to God and each other. We comfort and encourage one another, and we rejoice in our victories.

And we keep growing in grace together.

RESPONSE:

1. Have you experienced a safe community to pray with? How has it been a gift to you?
2. If not, are there safe people you could invite into a praying community with you?

DAY 90: A Gift of Gratitude

The pattern has been the same with all my grandkids. Whenever someone does something for a child, the parent says, "What do you say?"

The correct answer, of course, is "Thank you."

We humans aren't naturally grateful. It takes years of training for us to remember to say "Thank you" when someone is kind or helpful or generous to us.

We've just gone through a list of seven amazing gifts that God has given us through our prodigals, making your prodigal and mine the perfect gift for us.

Isn't it only right to say thank you to the Giver of this magnificent though challenging gift? Gratitude becomes our eighth gift.

God has observed, however, that we are much like children. He knows He must remind us often to say thank you.

But He takes it a lot further: "Give thanks in all circumstances; for this is God's will for you in Christ Jesus" (1 Thessalonians 5:18; see also Philippians 4:6; Ephesians 5:20).

And there we have it—the difficult command we pondered in chapter 4, "Rest," and again in chapter 5, "Trust": He wants us to thank Him *all* of the time, in *every* circumstance.

We've already acknowledged that thanking Him is easy when we like the circumstances of our lives, when we are healthy, have a good job, delight in loving relationships, have happy children, feel accepted and loved, experience success, receive a desired surprise. . . . At those times, the key is just to remember God is the Giver of all good things and to express gratitude.

But when health is threatened, a job is lost, a relationship is broken, children are making destructive choices, loneliness and rejection abound, success is elusive, and the surprises are not desired ones, how can we say thank you?

God asks us to. So we poise ourselves to learn how this is possible, how we can be motivated to even try thankfulness in hard times. In chapter 4, I shared three wonderful things that happen when I say, "Thank you, Lord": My focus changes, my trust expands, and doors open.

I want to further develop each of these thoughts.

My focus changes to God.

Giving thanks acknowledges He is God and He is good. When life circumstances are challenging, and yet I choose to say, "Thank you, Lord," I am saying to my heavenly Father, "I know you are God." I am recognizing that He is *El Elyon*, the Most High God, and He is *El Shaddai*, the Almighty. He is sovereign and over all, and in control.

But when life seems unfair, painful, confusing, scary, it is also important to remember He is good. Just look at these assurances of God's goodness:

- "I will make an everlasting covenant with them: I will never stop doing good to them, and I will inspire them to fear me, so that they will never turn away from me. I will rejoice in doing them good and will assuredly plant them in this land with all my heart and soul" (Jeremiah 32:40–41).
- "Taste and see that the LORD is good; blessed is the one who takes refuge in him" (Psalm 34:8).
- "You, Lord, are forgiving and good, abounding in love to all who call to you" (Psalm 86:5).

- "For the LORD is good and his love endures forever; his faithfulness continues through all generations" (Psalm 100:5).
- "You are good, and what you do is good; teach me your decrees" (Psalm 119:68).
- "The LORD is good to all; he has compassion on all he has made" (Psalm 145:9).

My trust expands. Giving thanks expresses trust in God. As we increasingly experience God's "Godness" and His goodness, we find our hearts and minds are more and more able to trust Him.

Fear—of all the uncertainties and concerns of life—erodes our trust. We find it harder to believe that God loves us and wants good for us. Learning to say thank you, even amidst pain and loss, restores our trust. We can go forward with confidence that we know who holds our future—and He knows, He cares, and He is able in every situation.

Doors open for God to work. Giving thanks opens opportunities for God to accomplish His heart's desires. I've found that, when hard circumstances restrain my gratitude, it's as though I am holding tightly to the key to my heart and the key to my circumstances. But when I thank God even when I don't feel thankful, it is like I hand Him the key to the locked door.

With that "thank you" key, He opens my eyes to begin to see the good He is doing, small though it may appear at first. He opens my mind to accept that His goodness will prevail, over time if not immediately. And that key opens my heart to restore trust that this all-powerful God is truly acting in love and compassion for me.

These three wonderful things have happened more and more frequently as I have intentionally practiced thanking God, as I have endeavored to make it a habit to grow a truly grateful heart.

I've worked on this over the years, in all I do, wherever I am, with whoever is watching. I know some of this attitude has transferred to my children. One of my favorite examples is this story: When our son joined our family at almost ten years old, life had dealt him some hard blows. Gratitude was not in him. We worked hard to teach him gratitude in general and especially toward God, even in hard times. Slowly, "thanks" became part of his vocabulary and even resided in his heart.

For many years he worked in landscaping, and once, while trimming a hedge by a fence with a chainsaw, the saw hit the fence and kicked back against his head, barely missing his eye and leaving a nasty gash.

When I got to the hospital and asked how he was, he said, "It hurts a lot. The first thing I did was call 9-1-1. The next thing I did was say, 'Thank you, Lord.'"

Again, I thank God for the gift of my prodigal.

I hope you will join me in saying it for *your* loved one: "Thank you, my God, for the incredible gift you have given me in my prodigal loved one."

RESPONSE:

1. Can you name some ways your loved one has been a gift to you?

2. What could help you to say "thank you" more consistently?

A Word from Josh

My early life was hard—bad things happened to me. As I got older I made a lot of bad choices: alcohol, drugs, girls, fights, lying, stealing. Why? Because it was fun, and my friends were doing all those things.

Eventually I grew tired of getting in trouble. I didn't want to go to jail. I began to see how stupid the things I was doing were. Maybe I was just growing up. But there were good people who loved me and spoke truth to me. There are still consequences today from some of my choices then.

Knowing God became important to me, especially talking to Him about everything. I read His Word—though reading it more would have been good—and I realized I needed to quit hanging out with people who led me astray and instead surround myself with better friends. Many people have prayed for me and loved me.

I am a different person in many ways now. My wife, Lesley, told me before we married that I had to quit drinking or she wouldn't marry me. I loved her, so I quit drinking. Growing up and encouragement from my wife helped me realize I wanted to be a good husband and father, and that required hard work and being responsible. It finally clicked what I needed to be and do.

If you love someone like me, remember that God is in control. He works it all in His plan. Keep affirming your prodigals and be firm with them. Look for good things to say, not just pointing out all they do wrong. Try to introduce them to people who will be good influences. Love them consistently.

And keep praying for them. I always want people to pray that I will keep walking straight. There are so many ways to step off the path. I need God's help to keep growing, working, and making right choices. So do your prodigals, wherever they are on their journeys.

A Word from Judy

If you love a prodigal, I am certain of this: Just as living through the prodigal wilderness journey has been one of the most transforming aspects of my life, so I believe it will be for you as well.

Seriously? Perhaps the words you would use would be *painful*, *scary*, *hurtful*, *demoralizing*, *immobilizing*. . . .

You see, I have lived through all the devotionals in this book.

What have I discovered? God is at work. Yes, in the lives of our loved prodigals—loving them, wooing them, revealing the emptiness of the lives they are pursuing, reminding them that you love them, arranging persuasive consequences, extending grace and mercy.

But I believe He has been equally—at least—at work in our lives, forming in us the likeness of Christ, revealing His love, mercy, and grace at depths we never knew before. We are realizing that the life He offers us is overflowing and abundant even when beset by pain and loss and fear. We have learned the power of prayer, the reality of intimacy with God himself, and the beauty of community with others.

And we are slowly comprehending that we can't do it. We ourselves can't live out love and grace and mercy as Jesus did. We can't make things happen the way we want, when we want. We lack the wisdom to know how to give to and guide, as well as restrain and correct, our wanderers. We aren't capable of the patience and per-severance required for this journey.

But our God knows that; *He* can do all that. And He lives in us through His Spirit, filling us and equipping us with supernatural power—to do the impossible.

And I am so grateful for the man Josh has become: kind, gentle, faithful, hardworking, generous, loving. He still has many challenges, but I gladly say, "Thank You, Lord, for Your good work in our son."

We may not know the end result—for our prodigals or ourselves—but our God promises, "Being confident of this, that he who began a good work in you will carry it on to completion until the day of Christ Jesus" (Philippians 1:6).

With Gratitude

This book has been written over more than a dozen years, so many have given to it and thus merit my gratitude.

The first one I must thank is God, who entrusted Josh to our family and walked with us every step of the way. He gave love, mercy, grace, wisdom, perseverance, and so much more to us on this wilderness journey.

Thank you, Joshua, for being such a teacher in the ways of God to us. You have provided many challenges, which turned out to be gifts. The story unfolds through the book.

Thank you, Steve, for being such a strong, faithful, encouraging, patient, and wise partner on this journey.

Debbie and Michelle, you also have been so much a part of this journey. Thank you for your grace and mercy to me and for your love for your brother.

Carla Kliever, my long-ago magazine partner, you have been a persistent, meticulous, and wise editor for every chapter.

Janet Kobobel Grant, also a long-ago magazine partner, founder of Books & Such Literary Management, and my agent: You encouraged me years ago to write this and helped me to prepare well to submit to publishers, with wonderful results. So here it is—thank you.

Three of my writer/editor friends were so kind to read the manuscript for me. Thank you, Maggie Bruehl, Kathy Horlacher, and Eloise Hatfield, for your diligent and discerning look at these words and for your wise counsel.

Numerous women in our Women's Resources office have helped in many ways: Susan Allendorf, Traci Anderson, Michelle Dodds, Lori Lloyd, Janey Nieboer, Sus Schmitt, Mary Smirnis, Anne Marie Winz.

Also thanks to Mick Haupt and Diego Cardenas for design work for early ebooks.

Jan Spoolstra, our years of history together totally equipped you to manage our team while I focused on writing. And many others have encouraged, prayed, brainstormed.

Special thanks goes to Wanda Rodriguez. She has typed, proofed, edited, proofed, typed, and prayed, so faithfully and excellently. She's the best proofreader I know, as well as prayer partner and encourager.

Faithful prayer warriors—on my personal prayer team and the Saucer Sisters—have prayed me through the long journey and now as I have written this book. Since I believe the work of God is done on our knees and then we see what He has done, this book is a result of their many prayers.

Tricia Beeber was a special listener and pray-er in the darkest days of the wilderness. Thank you. Susan Heckmann has been a constant encouragement.

The Prayer for Prodigals online community has been on this same journey. We have prayed for each other and our prodigals. These brave people have encouraged me and given me feedback and wisdom as I have written these devotionals over many years. Dena Yohe, thank you for your faithful partnership in guiding our group of prodigal lovers. Deborah Foxworth, Belinda Pastor, and Val Bush have helped us minister to many on this same journey.

My new friends at Bethany House Publishers have been wonderful to work with. Steve Oates, thank you for believing in this book.

Andy McGuire, you are a positive encourager and winsome guide. Paul Higdon, the cover is beautiful!! Sharon Hodge, I loved working with you on the edits—you are so insightful. As a grammar and proofreading geek myself, I am grateful for the good copy editing from Amanda Clawson. Kate Deppe, thanks for getting all those endorsements. Shaun Tabatt, thank you and your team—Chandler Carlson, Holly Maxwell, Sheridan Nelson—for making this book visible and desirable. Rod Jantzen and Adam Lorenz, I appreciate your efforts to get us into special places. Lucy Bixby, thanks for good service and attention to details.

Notes

Chapter 1: Love

1. "patient," Dictionary.com, https://www.dictionary.com/browse/patient.
2. "kind," Dictionary.com, https://www.dictionary.com/browse/kind?s=t.

Chapter 2: Grace

1. Thayer and Smith, "Greek Lexicon entry for Charis," *The NAS New Testament Greek Lexicon*, 1999, https://www.biblestudytools.com/lexicons/greek/nas/charis.html.
2. Josh Bales, "Only the Sinner," 2006. Used by permission.
3. John Newton, "Amazing Grace," 1772.
4. Charles R. Swindoll, "It's Time to Embrace Grace by Embracing the Unlovely," Insight for Living Ministries, June 15, 2009, https://www.insight.org/resources/article-library/individual/it%27s-time-to-embrace-grace-by-embracing-the-unlovely.
5. Swindoll, "It's Time to Embrace Grace."
6. Victor Hugo, *Les Misérables* (Brussels, Belgium: A. Lacroix, Verboeckhoven & Cie, 1862).
7. Philip Yancey, *What's So Amazing About Grace?* (Grand Rapids, MI: Zondervan Publishing House, 1997), 88–90.
8. Henri Nouwen, *The Return of the Prodigal Son: A Story of Homecoming* (New York: Doubleday Image Books, 1992), 129–130.
9. Yancey, *What's So Amazing About Grace?*, 93.

Chapter 3: Time

1. Hannah Hurnard, *Hinds' Feet on High Places* (Hannah Hurnard, 1988).
2. Mark Batterson, *The Circle Maker: Praying Circles Around Your Biggest Dreams and Greatest Fears* (Grand Rapids, MI: Zondervan Publishing House, 2016).
3. Mark Batterson, *Draw the Circle: The 40 Day Prayer Challenge* (Grand Rapids, MI: Zondervan Publishing House, 2012), 110–112.

Chapter 4: Rest

1. Used by permission. *For the Family*, Sylvia Gunter ©The Father's Business, P.O. Box 380333, Birmingham, AL 35238, www.thefathersbusiness.com. All rights reserved.

Chapter 5: Trust

1. Brennan Manning, *Ruthless Trust: The Ragamuffin's Path to God* (New York: Harper Collins, 2010).
2. Manning, *Ruthless Trust*, 52.
3. Hannah Hurnard, *Hinds' Feet on High Places* (Hannah Hurnard, 1988).
4. Tim Keller, *The Reason for God: Belief in an Age of Skepticism* (London: Penguin Books, 2009).
5. Tim Keller, "My Faith: The Danger of Asking God 'Why Me?'" *CNN Belief Blog*, August 4, 2012, http://religion.blogs.cnn.com/2012/08/04/my-faith-the-danger-of-asking-god-why-me/.
6. "Oh the Deep, Deep Love of Jesus," by S. Trevor Francis, 1875.
7. Manning, *Ruthless Trust*, 24.
8. Manning, *Ruthless Trust*, 33.
9. Manning, *Ruthless Trust*, 37.
10. Manning, *Ruthless Trust*, 37.

Chapter 6: Prayer

1. John Ortberg, *Soul Keeping: Caring for the Most Important Part of You* (Grand Rapids, MI: Zondervan Publishing House, 2014).
2. Ortberg, *Soul Keeping*, 23.
3. 1 Corinthians 13:12 KJV. "For now we see through a glass, darkly; but then face to face: now I know in part; but then shall I know even as also I am known."
4. Romans 2:4. "Or do you show contempt for the riches of his kindness, forbearance and patience, not realizing that God's kindness is intended to lead you to repentance?"

Chapter 7: Promise

1. "Daniel 4," *Matthew Henry Commentary on the Whole Bible*, www.biblestudytools.com/commentaries/matthew-henry-complete/daniel/4.html.

Chapter 8: Hope

1. James Strong, "Psalm 27:13–14" in *The Hebrew Bible*, Authorized English Version (Cedar Rapids, Iowa: Laridian Electronic Files, 2005).
2. Dena Yohe, *You Are Not Alone: Hope for Hurting Parents of Troubled Kids* (Colorado Springs, CO: WaterBrook, 2016), 66.

Resources

Books:

Alcoholics Anonymous, *The Big Book* (New York: Alcoholics Anonymous World Services, 2001).

Nancy Alcorn, *Cut: Mercy for Self-Harm* (Enumclaw, WA: Winepress, 2007).

Nancy Alcorn, *Starved: Mercy for Eating Disorders* (Enumclaw, WA: Winepress, 2007).

Neil Anderson, *The Bondage Breaker* (Eugene, OR: Harvest House Publishers, 2006).

Neil Anderson, *Steps to Freedom in Christ* (Bloomington, MN: Bethany House, 2017).

Neil Anderson, *Victory Over the Darkness: Realizing the Power of Your Identity in Christ*, 10th Anniversary ed. (Raleigh, NC: Regal, 2000).

James Banks, *Prayers for Prodigals: 90 Days of Prayer for Your Child* (Grand Rapids, MI: RBC Ministries, 2011).

Allison Bottke, *Setting Boundaries with Your Adult Children: Six Steps to Hope and Healing for Struggling Parents* (Eugene, OR: Harvest House, 2008).

Mark Bubeck, *The Adversary: The Christian Versus Demon Activity* (Chicago: Moody Publishers, 2013).

Henry Cloud and John Townsend, *Boundaries: When to Say Yes, When to Say No to Take Control of Your Life* (Grand Rapids, MI: Zondervan, 1992).

Sharron Cosby, *Praying for Your Addicted Loved One: 90 in 90* (Auburn, WA: BookJolt, 2013).

Larry Crabb, *Shattered Dreams: God's Unexpected Pathway to Joy* (Colorado Springs, CO: WaterBrook, 2001).

Nancy Guthrie, *Holding on to Hope: A Pathway through Suffering to the Heart of God* (Wheaton, IL: Tyndale, 2002).

Sharon Hersh, *The Last Addiction: Why Self Help Is Not Enough, Own Your Desire, Live Beyond Recovery, Find Lasting Freedom* (Colorado Springs, CO: WaterBrook, 2008).

Timothy Keller, *Walking with God through Pain and Suffering* (New York: Dutton, 2013).

Carol Kent, *A New Kind of Normal: Hope-Filled Choices When Life Turns Upside Down* (Nashville, TN: Thomas Nelson, 2007).

Carol Kent, *When I Lay My Isaac Down: Unshakable Faith in Unthinkable Circumstances* (Colorado Springs, CO: NavPress, 2004).

Jim Logan, *Reclaiming Surrendered Ground: Protecting Your Family from Spiritual Attacks* (Chicago: Moody, 1995).

Robert J. Morgan, *Moments for Families with Prodigals* (Colorado Springs, CO: NavPress, 2003).

Sarah H. Nielsen, *Just Keep Going: Spiritual Encouragement from the Mom of a Troubled Teen* (Maitland, FL: Xulon Press, 2011).

Stormie Omartian, *The Power of a Praying Parent*, Reprint ed. (Eugene, OR: Harvest House, 2014).

Omartian, *The Power of Praying for Your Adult Children*, Reprint ed. (Eugene, OR: Harvest House, 2014).

Brendan O'Rourke and DeEtte Sauer, *The Hope of a Homecoming: Entrusting Your Prodigal to a Sovereign God* (Colorado Springs, CO: NavPress, 2003).

Janet Thompson, *Praying for Your Prodigal Daughter: Hope, Help & Encouragement for Hurting Parents* (New York: Howard Books, 2007).

John Vawter, ed. *Hit by a Ton of Bricks: You're Not Alone When Your Child's on Drugs* (Little Rock, AR: Family Life Publishing, 2003).

John White, *Parents in Pain: A Book of Comfort and Counsel* (Downers Grove, IL: InterVarsity, 1979).

Philip Yancey, *Disappointment with God: Three Questions No One Asks Aloud* (New York: Harper Collins, 1988).

Renee Yohe, *Purpose for the Pain: A Collection of Journals* (Orlando, FL: Bonded Books, 2008).

Websites:

About Alcoholism: www.aboutalcoholism.net

Al-Anon: www.al-anon.org

Breakthrough: www.intercessors.org

Celebrate Recovery: www.celebraterecovery.com

Co-Dependents Anonymous: www.coda.org

Deeper Walk International: Resources by Mark Bubeck at www.deeper-walk-international.myshopify.com

Nar-Anon: www.nar-anon.org

The Prodigal Hope Network: www.partnersinprayerforourprodigals.com

Prayer for Prodigals, developed by Cru (formerly Campus Crusade for Christ), request invitation via email: PrayerforProdigals@gmail.com

National Suicide Prevention Lifeline: www.suicideprevention lifeline.org and 1-800-273-8255 (TALK); call 24/7, 365 days a year, including holidays.

Judy Douglass is the founder and host of Prayer for Prodigals, an online community for those who love someone who is making destructive choices. She has served as editor of two Cru (Campus Crusade for Christ) magazines, has authored five books, and speaks all over the world. A writer, speaker, encourager, and advocate, Judy loves to encourage God's children to be and do all that He created them for. A native of Dallas, she graduated from the University of Texas with a degree in journalism. Judy serves as director of Cru's Women's Resources and partners with her husband, Steve, president of Campus Crusade for Christ International, to lead Cru globally. Judy and Steve live in Orlando, Florida.